Innocence in a Sense

the Stuff of Me

Mitchell W Bennett BFA, BSW

First Published 2022 by Mitchell Bennett
Copyright © Mitchell Bennett BFA BSW 2022
All rights reserved. No part of this publication may be reproduced or transmitted in any form or by any means, electronic or mechanical, including photocopying, recording or any information storage or retrieval system, without prior permission in writing from the publishers.

ISBN: 978-0-6454362-7-3
Cover art by Mitchell Bennett.
Typesetting and cover design by Rack & Rune Publishing
rackandrune.com

Contents

Prologue	5
Off the Freeway	9
Into My Heart and Mind	19
Rambling Along Purposely	29
No Time to Spare, and Then …	35
My Spirit Beckons: Good Timing and Safe Taming	49
A Vigorous All-Rounder: Rough and Ready to Play	69
Begone My Mind Adrift … Begin the Forming of My Faith	81
Caution the Ripple Which Can Lead to the Riptide	97
Moral Compass and Misdemeanours	105
Deeper and Down	113
A Bit of a Mess	121
Digging Myself Out of the Hole	129
The Wordsmith at Work, the Decision to Write	141
The Golden Fleece of Wellbeing	155
Acknowledgements:	161
References	165

Prologue

The sound of a small fixed-wing airplane drones high in the sky as I sit hunched on the side of the bed. My hands clasp my forehead, and my thoughts are clouded. A small beam of light peeps through the slit in the heavy blue curtains that cover my windows. Their old wooden frames are my gateway of vision into the large backyard. I stare, reflecting on everything this wonderland has offered: family gatherings, soccer, cricket, footy and hours of splashing around in the vinyl-lined, metal-capped pool. Endless fun and happy days.

I am shut off from the outside world, entombed. The colourful walls of yellow and turquoise that were painted by my brother, Stuart, are shadowed now. I know it is late morning because of the ever-present, stuffy humidity and heat in the room. It has stirred me out from under the covers. I am uncomfortable, sweaty, my mind a haze. The toilet flushes, a familiar sound coming from the bathroom that adjoins my bedroom.

I know I am not alone in the house but remain frozen in a trance-like state. Time has no concept for me. I remain in this defeated position. Sitting crouched, waiting … I am in a state of darkness and confusion, time passing without trace. I strain to comprehend what time is. Five minutes or several hours?

***

Desperately though gently, I am coerced out of the back seat of Mum's trusty 1970s Holden Torana. It is a safe refuge I cannot manage to leave as I hold tight to the door, gripping fiercely. I am indecisive and fearful of what is next; it is an out of body experience. The voices of my mother and aunt are kind, but with a persistent sense of urgency.

"Come out, Mitchell."

"Come on, it's all right, luv."

The request is repeated over and over.

There is a faint sense of familiarity; I know these grounds. This unexpected visit sends caution through the core of me. My mother and aunt lure me into a concrete bunker of a building. My confusion takes on an urgency, as time is lost. I am walking through a maze-like walkway, and the arched, corrugated roof blocks out the fading afternoon sun. A large, firmly clenched hand presses the back of my neck like a massive weight. I am driven forward metre by metre, my head facing downward towards the grey concrete path.

The dominant, alien hand is oppressive. I can hear

no other voices. Where are comforting instructions or explanations of what is happening? I may have stopped muttering and groaning. The forced march is done in the complete silence of defeat. I give in to the pressure on the back of my neck with the noose-like grip. I look down on myself as an object, barely considering where I am being taken. As I surrender, I am lost.

***

This account is of my fifteen-year-old self, trapped in my first psychosis and admission to hospital. I have hungered to tell my story, reaching back to the past when my young voice was on the verge of breaking. The breaking voice was coupled with a broken mind. It has taken many years of healing. Healing is a constant state, as is recovery.

Now I talk with an occasionally crackling, older, and wiser voice. I hope that the experiences outlined in the story that follows, and the memories of the difficult life stages interspersed with joy, may serve others who have struggled or are struggling now. These words provide insight into my life as a young person who experienced the onset of serious mental illness. As I walk through the gamut of both happy and turbulent experiences, I expose hurts, but hopefully I balance these with a sense of hope. Older and wiser now, I am telling this story for the first time.

1
Off the Freeway

My father died suddenly at the age of forty-one. Family holidays after Frank Bennett's death were not easy. The tsunami of shock immediately after the loss meant an adjustment to new routines for Mum and the many people in our lives. It was beyond difficult, but my brothers and I were largely sheltered due to our ages and the distractions of the extended family. I would add that we did get to experience many memorable times though in my infant years.

Borenore—located just out of Orange, a country city in the Central Tablelands of New South Wales— became a favourite family holiday destination for some years. Today, Orange is referenced as a major regional location. Back in the 1970s, however, it was more of a country town, with that feel of real escape into the outback. Rich farming land through and through, burgeoning with cherries in the spring. And it was here our family relatives on my Pa's side welcomed us. This was the farm property where the legendary Bradleys resided.

We set out to Borenore, and the homestead called "Jindalee," home of Clyde, Nora and the Bradley offspring. It took us the whole day in Mum's Kingswood to get there. Well, so it seemed to a toddler. At the crack of dawn, we were wedged into the car half asleep. Pillows and blankets padded us, buffeting us from suitcases and each other, should any spontaneous fighting erupt. We trekked west of Sydney through Windsor, up the winding road through the Blue Mountains. The sweet sound of bellbirds chimed, beckoning welcome to the bush escarpment. Up and over the Great Dividing Range we motored on. The temperature was cool, and fog masked our vision. Mum, a sturdy and confident driver, navigated the maze-like roads like a bullet finding its target.

We would stop for a break somewhere down on the flat plains, with the mountain range at our backs, in a remote town along the way. Our travel hamper contained fruit and sandwiches, the obligatory favourites: peanut butter and jam. Several hours from home, we breathed in the cool, fresh country air, edged with the smells of animals unique to the farmland regions.

With a top up of petrol, we were on our way again. Wide awake now, the second part of the road trip contained some distraction from the droning of the car engine. "Guess and know" books were the favourite form of entertainment. They contained puzzles, dot-to-dot drawings and word games that would spark curiosity on every page. I particularly liked the special felt-tipped pen you could use to swipe over a line in invisible ink to reveal the answer, as magic came forth.

Our anticipation would steadily grow as we approached our destination. Conversation would break out, usually initiated by my older brothers. Their memories of this wonderland were discussed with great enthusiasm. The school holidays we were now enjoying sparked delight and intrigue of the adventures that awaited us.

Grrrr, grrrr, the tyres sang, as the slowing car began bumping over the cattle grate. Down the long, dirt driveway we would edge closer. We were finally here at Jindalee! I remember the homestead in full view, and the paddock to the right, where the old brown bull stood. His strong self of presence and his high status were reflected in his white patched markings, giving him prized notoriety. He stood contemptuously, staring down at these newcomers to the farm. We were warned, yet again, "Never go into his paddock," and felt the young boys' drawing of temptation.

Arriving, we were greeted with smiles, hugs and kisses from the family. Numerous friendly cats swirled around our legs, making their mark on us. The working dogs, all lined up, flanking a corridor to the chook house, were barking and dashing left to right with excitement. Each one was chained to their rustic kennel, stirring up the dust enthusiastically as they responded to our arrival. Anticipation of the experiences of farm life was both eagerly awaited, and simultaneously confronting. Full of interesting machinery, animals and farm sheds, the farm also had an eeriness about it, a strangeness, I thought to myself. I pondered as a small child of the farm tasks that took place in those sheds.

We settled in for the night after our long road trip that day. The next morning at 5.45am, pitch dark before the sunrise, farm life sprang into action. In a daze, we rose from our cots and beds, slipped on trousers, woolly jumpers, mittens, beanies and gum boots in preparation for the morning routine. *Squirt, squirt, squirt,* as milk flowed into the metal bucket standing under the udder of this jersey mum, the steady stream splashing the sides of the bucket. With a quick flick of one teat, Uncle Clyde would splash one of the cats in the face. At the ready with open mouth, the black and white cat would catch a full dose.

Following this first job, it was back into the farmhouse for our own tasty treats. The spread that Aunty Nora had prepared exhibited about every homemade delight you can think of. I experienced the definition of what really constituted a "big breakfast." My favourite was the fresh-made cream with homemade blackberry jam on toast.

The day ahead would involve riding on the tractor, herding sheep from one paddock to another, where more grazing could be had. Clyde would keep an eye out for any menacing crows on the lookout for vulnerable lambs. The cry of a crow still gives me shudders today. They could peck the eyes from the defenceless little lamb. Awful. Returning to the hay shed, we would then take the truck loaded with hay bales down the well-worn tracks to spend the rest of the morning until lunch feeding the cattle and checking fences.

Uncle Clyde's unique calling to muster the cattle was a low-pitched sound of "Come-on, come-on," like a human foghorn. The cattle seemed to know exactly what this meant. And of course, they could see the stack of tasty lucerne piled up on the back of the truck. Our job was to break apart the bales and, in biscuits (hand-width portions), hurl them to the ground, forming a trail of food for the cows. Dusty hard work, but such fun.

After another feed, a "big lunch" this time, more farm activities took place. What time or season we would visit dictated the various farm activities. Clyde, Nora and the kids were a family made up of "Jack of all's" or, put another way, a Renaissance family. In this way, they were able to do most things farm life commanded. All year round. This taught me the importance of adaptability, even as a small child.

For fun we would ride, perched on huge, beautiful horses Pye and Ringo, much loved pets of the family. My brother

Andrew experienced the ride of his life when, suddenly, the horse was spooked by something, and Ringo bolted into full canter. "Hold, hold on," Clyde screamed, as Andrew clung tightly with both fists in Ringo's mane. The ride seemed to only last moments, as Clyde cornered the animal and, with stern yet soothing calling of "Whoo boy, whoo boy," quickly grabbed the reins. Uncle Clyde was able to bring Ringo to a halt. Little Andrew had performed like a professional jockey, race-ready position, hardly sitting in the saddle. He had survived.

After risk-ridden adventures, the end of the day begun: digging for earth worms, as each wriggling beauty was gathered in a bucket. We now had bait for our fishing activity upon dusk. Yellowfin were stocked in the enormous freshwater dam in the rear paddock. With fishing rods in hand, a bucket of worms, and luck on our side, we would stroll down the same worn pathway as we had driven down earlier in the day, climb under the barbwire fence, and position ourselves for the catch.

However, the job was made easy for us. Uncle Clyde would cast a line into the middle of the dam, and then prop up the rod into a Y-shaped stick which he pushed into the ground. The same process was completed with the other four rods. In the morning we would return to a fine catch of four fish. These were then frozen and sent home with us as bounty.

As evening came, and the sun descended behind Mt Canobolas in the distant west, we would retire for the day at the homestead. However not before the preparation of sloshing soup and bone mix, which was dog food. The nutritious meal would be dished out to each worker dog, a reward for all the effort accompanying us that day. Two scoops of coke (a form of coal) for the evening slow combustion fireplace would be gathered and lugged into the house. Finally, we would retreat into the cosy dwelling. Our warm home away from home.

After the day's work, an almighty feast awaited us. Nora's culinary delights would be served in such a spread, satisfying each of our rumbling bellies. Moving into the lounge room after dinner, the evening news hour would be screening on the black and white Rank Arena TV. Usually by seven- thirty or so, you could hear Uncle Clyde snoring as he stretched out in his armchair, legs crossed with a woolly pair of socks just visible from under his dirt-stained trousers. His snoring played the tune of a familiar sounding rumble, punctuating the end of a routine hard day's work.

Action-oriented holidays on the farm with the Bradleys provided respite as a family away from city life. Those school holiday breaks seemed endless. We were so fortunate to have such positive periods of learning outside of the suburban life in Sydney. Clyde and Nora did not understand, until years later, how much they helped shape all of us Bennett boys. The words of truth spoken, physical activity and wise mentoring made these holidays unique. I grew up over the years wanting too to be a Renaissance man, as I remembered the lessons taught to me as a small boy.

By way of winding this holiday experience down, and this first chapter, I relay a more recent experience of my own family.

The title of this chapter is a phrase that was used often by my children: "Off the freeway," my two boys would chant. Concluding our road trip in our family car, from the back seat, their piercing voices would be heard. When this practice began, they were not able to read. As the years went on, they were able to interpret the massive green freeway signs as their reading skills improved. Our turn off was wrapped close by with the familiar surrounding mountain ranges. The mood of the mountains filled up the car windows as we approached our turn off.

The faded blue-grey vista reflected the easy going, sleepy little town this day. On another day, a dark green and black menacing landscape would indicate that there had been rain, and that dampness abounded. Heaviness. A mood of happiness on other occasions was mirrored in the serene detail of the approaching trees. In whatever way each of us were reminded of our surroundings through such landmarks, we all knew we were only moments from concluding our trip, safely in the comfort of our own home. We had ventured away, only to return to the familiar which grounded us. Much like the holiday ventures and return trips to the Bennett family home of my childhood days.

Now, the difference is that the young men in our family unit love pumping music or sitting in complete silence while they use their mobile devices. These are distractions from the familiar landmarks. But there is still a sense of coming home, which is treasured. Road trips are still something to look forward to. It was good to go exploring and travel, but the healing found in returning home once more was just as good.

2
Into My Heart and Mind

The serenity that home brings upon each returning trip is a powerful reminder that home is where my heart is. More importantly, home is also where my mind lives. Heart and mind combined and were in balance with each other. My definition of home is comprised of two parts. The first is the physical building and its contents where I can relax comfortably. This place is full of restoration, and rejuvenation. Life-giving fun exists there, building a wall against trials and tribulations, all shared with my family. We have created a positive space, warm in winter and cool in summer, to allow escape from the summer heat. Home is a place where we learn from each other, as we come and go with our daily activities. Home is much more than just a shared house.

The second home I will refer to within this book is a place of "coming home" in my own mind. A metaphorical place of desired peace. To be at one with myself in my thinking is welcomed. In this space, there is respite and retreat from turmoil. This state of mind is always being worked on too, much the same as a family home needs upkeeping. Keeping a state of a healthy mind requires maintenance in several creative ways. I require both skills and tools to keep my "personal home" functional. My mind habitat requires specific things. To look after me. To keep my wellbeing. And this state of mind must be a functional and healing place, so that creativity can flow, and there is an outpouring of myself.

There can be a tension between "being home" and the imperative to journey. This book, based on many years of journaling, is my road map. The metaphor of a road trip explains my journey leading up to the adult age of nineteen. From then on, the story proceeds as if on a surf safari. I am now in my fifties, but started journaling at eighteen, and explored my childhood and youth. My voice has been carried through the journal until now. Many of the insights I have been given have arisen through stream of consciousness writing. I have reflected on the previous years, and on how my primary and juvenile years provided many opportunities for personal growth. Through my younger years, the choices that have impacted me at each challenge have led to both positive and negative outcomes.

The impact of the different communities that have touched me is profound, and there are key individuals who have influenced such decision making. Many would not have realised the influence they have had on me. When making my decisions these individuals have unknowingly contributed to the many twists and turns of these formative and special years.

The ultimate vehicle for any surf safari up the East Coast of Australia in the eighties and nineties was the Kingswood. No bias here of course. It was an inspirational car, a massive tank of a thing, greedy for petrol after a few kilometres. As I changed gears often with the "three on the tree" (three speed manual column shift), I was careful not to jam the linkage. With the wind whistling into the cabin, through every crack and rust hole, I drove on.

The road trip helps me think of life as a journey. Free and easy at times, though along the way I encountered rough terrain, hard going periods, and went off the beaten track at times. I began my scribblings as raw material for a book by way of my journals. During road trips back then, my journaling would be a key activity when stopping at each surf break. A real surf safari. I surfed breaks and, in between, grabbed hamburgers and thick shakes or made a service station Slurpee stop when it was hot. I have now written volumes. In every place I have visited. I have been preparing myself for the task of writing this book.

At eighteen, I already had the attitude of just get out there and live life, wish for your own future, take chances, and make every choice worthwhile. The same as paddling in on a wave. You have a moment when you either commit and take off on the face of the wave, or you falter, pull off the back, or risk getting taken over the falls. Wipe out!

Both apply to the surfing experience, and to life. That is, sometimes you make it, other times you do not, or cannot, for a range of reasons. I was learning at eighteen what it took to be a mature adult. I hark back to those days as wonderful and carefree. I only had a cloudy image of what I would like to be in later years as an adult. I lived in the now and enjoyed life one day at a time. Throughout, returning home—after any road trip, long or short, at whatever age—was inextricably linked to returning home safe and sound in my mind.

My number line analogy comes into play here. What I mean is that my writing style can appear a bit like leaping forward, with smaller jumps back, only to pause and leap forward again. Bouncing around without structure. Years of journal writing may have something to do with this. As I have reflected upon my writing style, I tend to launch forward to current events, then swing back in time ever so quickly again. I know at times I also change tense too easily. If you imagine a straight line as the baseline: that's not me! Draw an arc forward several points. Then draw another arc back a couple of points, landing at a different point along the base line. Well, that is how this story is pictured and progresses with me. However, I am always making ground. Some big jumps forward about the life and times of Mitch, and smaller jumps back to earlier events too. Picture this mental imagery as it unfolds over the coming pages. I try to make sense of things, in my own way. I hope you get the gist! Email me upon finishing the book, and I'll explain it further!

The examples of childhood experiences shared within these chapters occur in many different places, though springboard from a loving home environment. My experiences have mostly led to positive results. However, not all have done so. Looking back, I posed the question to myself: How did I come to make the choices I made for myself? At what age in my developing years was I truly responsible for them? When did I learn to live comfortably with the outcomes?

I did get lost on one occasion in my teens. This period in my life had devastating consequences that have lasted a lifetime. I took a couple of wrong turns, where I was faced with serious choices. Ultimately, I learned that "every choice is worth your while," as it simply leads to another choice. You may get lost, but you can find yourself again. That's the bit of wisdom I impart here. Mostly, I have managed to find my way back to a safe place again. Getting lost was no fun. Though using my own personal resources, I was able to work my way back to the track again. This is where the journey came alive. Lost, then found again, is a key theme throughout this book.

The event I am alluding to was my deep dive in mental health illness. And how I learnt to swim through the literal highs and lows. It has been a roller-coaster ride, and there is no getting off. Accepting this has been huge. My management of myself through the exhilarating peaks, and the ever-looming dips, brought trembling fear and horror. I thought this would be my lot forever. By extending my hand for help, I have received life-giving support along the way. Doorways have opened in every aspect of my life. I question myself: Why did this happen? Was it through luck, or by design?

So, drive with me as a passenger in the Kingswood "Woody" for a bit. Let me convince you that every choice is worth your while, as you journey through your own arc-making process too.

As I draw each arc along the timeline of my life, I can see that digging deep and finding the embryonic wisdom within, or my early adult voice at this life stage, was a key feature that moved me to the light. As a young person, as I hopped on the roller coaster of life, I took a firm grip. I had to!

I found out early that having a friend, relative, partner—or self—living with the experience of mental illness is common. If you haven't heard another's story, then let me be your first metaphorical traveller friend to share my insights on life. Maybe there is a lost and found story in you.

Putting it out there is a form of therapy and healing which has led me in new directions. As any safari would have it, I have developed a pattern in my life of detouring down those winding roads. Not lost, just diverted.

Freeways or motorways are one mode of road travel where cars, motorbikes and trucks travel, soaking up large distances between a start point and a destination. All over the world there are different examples, of such roadways. In Australia, where I live, you can literally travel for days to reach your destination. The scenery in Australia, leaving city life behind, often becomes more uniform in its vast geography. Open rolling landscapes with slow-changing appearances drift seemingly by. A travelling experience without the need to focus on much of the detail. A steady rolling of the wheels, a monotonous droning of the engine. An acceptance of the wind rushing past any extremity of the vehicle. When on a motor bike, wind turbulence remains as a fierce reminder of your vulnerability among the elements. For the driver/rider, there's anticipation for each kilometre passing, the destination slowly drawing closer. The job was to harmonise with the conditions. It starts with a feeling of fleeing, and freedom. The escape has been made. We are on the freeway.

This can morph into a different way of thinking,

perceiving time and space in a new way. The constant reminder is that this is a new beginning. Large expanses of time. My time. And on this journey with you as my passenger, we can swap thoughts and ideas, and create a shared experience. Our destination is relatively uncharted at this point. But we need to hang on. I knew at nineteen that asking for help was behind my own success. And as I have come to witness, the most successful people through life have reached out to others along the way.

I learned to drive a car at sixteen. But in contrast to freeway driving, open spaces, and galloping kilometres are the "off the freeway" routes: the back street, where the twisting and turning experience of journeying compare life's macro scenery to more detailed accounts of rich complexities, through suburbs of towns and cities along the way. Landscapes or detailed scenes brimming with a different kind of energy and spilling frantic displays of busyness at every corner. A feeling of warp speed as I exhale the pressure to be somewhere fast.

To write *The Stuff of Me* is unique to me. I did display innocence, in a sense, as I experienced my own juvenile years. It tipped me through a series of hairpin turns, at times harrowing experiences. I was able to reorient and reinvent myself time and again. Sometimes, I was on pathways to small successes, while other times there were rich life lessons. I was never truly alone, and mostly never felt existentially alone. Though I have frequented many lonely places along the way, I have met loners too. I love them.

3
Rambling Along Purposely

My number line analogy is at play here as I begin this chapter. It is an important leap forward, I feel, at this early stage.

From over twenty-five years of journaling, I found comfort in speaking my mind, with no rules, through a bound notebook and pen. This anchored me while experiencing some hellish rides. Think of riding a bike. Sometimes the biggest thrills are the downhill runs, where your eyes seep with tears from the exhilaration and rush combined. The only thing to do is to hang on tight, keep your instinctual balance, and pray it would be alright. Once the experience is in the past and safety reigns, you can evaluate things. The battle with the moods I experienced parallels this: speed of thought, the wild ride, and a crash. Time to rest forced upon me.

I am still here, telling the story. I have evaluated many roller-coaster rides. I am currently residing safely, which has made it possible to finish this book. An altered mind state is full of turmoil. It is not a holiday escape. Returning to a clear and healthy state of mind is a thing greatly to be desired after psychosis. But it takes courage to find your way home.

The notion of adventure beckoned in my mid-teens. The imperative I recognise for myself now is to move forward, not get lost in the past, or stay bogged, but release myself, "from myself." I glance at the landscape behind me, which helped me focus on the direction I choose to go in. Only by looking at history can I envisage the future. Moving forward and responding to change is a good thing. A fact: no landscape stays the same.

As I have journeyed some distance through life now, I ask myself how certain memories gain their power. Each memory I recalled served as a significant snapshot of who I was at a specific life stage. It led me to reveal "the stuff of me," quintessentially. Similarly, being told, "just follow your nose," was taken to heart, like a lot of things as a child. I was old enough to know it as a joke, but my nose *has* been a compass of sorts, as I sniffed out directions that have suited me. The use of my other senses has come into play too. I learnt what I needed to hear, as I fully comprehended contexts. I felt my way around, and looked with keen eyes at the world, as I savoured the bittersweet moments. I came to my "senses" early on in life.

One nickname I achieved mid-teens was in fact "Wombat Nose." Make of it what you will. More than one person identified the wombat as having a lot in common with me. I like to think it was a term of affection given to me from my peers, that, indeed, I was considered a cute and a cuddly sort of fellow. However, I am pretty sure the nickname was given to me because of my physical features. I have a unique nose. Put it that way. Whatever the sentiment, it didn't bother me. It was far better than some of the other ones used during those high school days.

Travel is my metaphor, and the use of a variety of modes of transport demonstrates my journey. From early beginnings, my modes of transport have been an amazing progression. Beginning with the infant: bum slide, knees, toppled feet, baby bouncer, dinky, tod rod. Then the scooter, push bike, minibike, BMX and racing bike, trail bike, roller skates, ice skates, skateboard, sailboat, surfboard, wind surfer. And advancing to the jet ski, land sailor, grass skis, snow skis, road motorbike, enduro motorbike, power boat and, of course, the many varieties of cars. Hoh yes, the many cars!

I am sure I can add to this list even more. I learnt through all these modes of transport that performing circles is not truly forward motion. Circle work, a term known to motor enthusiasts, just leaves more and more impressions of donuts. Or ruts in the ground. Or rubber on the road. And, to the mariners among us, it is possible to leave more wake in the waves through wasted effort. Some elements of fun—yes. Definitely. Though, in some cases, I was propelled head-on into a crash zone a few times. Staring cross-eyed did not help when looking down your nose. There was more required than just following your nose, I found out. A compass in life is a good thing.

The journey thus far has taken me through valleys, and over mountains, through seas, and over the airways. There was tough terrain, high and low swell conditions, and turbulent pockets. However, explaining such experiences has brought me meaning. The reasons will unfold all in good time, revealed in the following chapters. Wherever you find yourself reading this, I hope you're "at home" with yourself.

Well, I'm not implying you must be "at home" to read this: you could be on a train or plane, but still be mostly in a healthy mental state. A safe and healing place of your own. If times, mentally, are challenging for you, I want to bring a sense of hope into your life. I have placed a welcome mat down. I invite you to share my head space for a while. Join me in the Kingswood. I hope to make the trip entertaining. Life is too short for doom and gloom. Buckle up for the metaphorical trip.

You might begin to see some examples of landscapes or seascapes that remind you of your travels so far. You may just chill out, put your feet up on the dash; the Kingswood is perfect for that. Take it all in. This journey may kickstart something new in your mind. You may find your own compass or begin sketching a different framework and design for your own home in your head and heart. From that healthy state, anything is possible. I just want to pass on some tips along the way, in making sense of this world.

In this life journey, I have built in my mind a resilient framework. It took time and effort, and the development of a real work ethic. Sweat, blood and tears. On the inside, we are all master builders—a reference I use, thanks to *The Lego Movie*, released a few years back. Emmet and the Wyldstyle/Lucy are lead characters. Both are "special," and together they find this out.

From a very early age, I imagined something of my adult life. In my teen years, this image was further developed. I never thought I would make it to this life stage, but I was sustained by my dreams from very early beginnings. Hope played a big part in my expectation of life's outcomes. I mostly wanted to be a young dad. At thirty-three, I experienced being a dad for the first time. Then again at thirty-five. I believe I was young at heart.

The ongoing role of parenthood now is beautiful beyond belief. It is the gift that keeps giving, and each time I leave the house through the gate at the bottom of the driveway, I give thanks. As I reflect over the years spent at our property, I cherish the infant voices of our boys that I can still recall, as I refer in the opening lines, within the chapter "Off the

Freeway," where I describe our travelling experiences back to our home. I can still hear each of them. Squeaky little things their voices were. Emotion surges through me every time I recall them.

I have a painting hanging up in my shed. I painted this canvas which I titled "Dream Nightmare." It is indeed the front cover of this book. It was one of my self-reflection projects early in my Fine Arts degree. It represents the broken figure of my youth that was able to be pieced together. Patched up. It represented the sixteen-year-old me. Yet, I could see the man in me too. During the years of my life, I have had my share of nightmares. But these have been balanced by many joys.

4
No Time to Spare, and Then …

A dog's life is seven years to each human year. When I was told that my dog Tess would live to about twelve by the vet, this really meant, in human years that she would live to eighty-four years old. A once in a lifetime companion. I have captured the memory of her in this book. She had many adventures, between trips down the back, hooning down to the beach, beloved dinner times, resting on the mat and, of course, chastising Odie, our other dog. She taught me that, essentially, life is short. However, you can pack in a terrible amount into each year. Between the ages of sixteen and nineteen, I seemed to do just that. And I grew up at rather a rapid rate.

I have lived for many years beyond nineteen now. At nineteen, I accepted the adult world. I had some idea of what I was in for, and then again, I did not. Reliving it as I write this has been satisfying and cathartic. No one has my arm twisted behind my back; it is of my wanting and doing. By doing this, I have felt that I have experienced my childhood and teen years at warp speed, faster than at any other decade. What was crammed into those first formative years took me beyond my own maturity. I was forced to confront aspects of myself I never asked for. But the solid childhood footing formed the foundation for me to live through my turbulent teens, and beyond.

Middle age presents a whole other story. Life, although still busy, leads to a slight slowing of time. It takes me longer to do things now, but I can afford this luxury. With the aging process well established, I am reminded about the forces of gravity: joint pain, cracked skin, browning teeth and grey hair. They confirm my merely mortal status and keep me grounded these days. And the desire to retire early of an evening is pleasing to the soul.

Back to the foundations of childhood. It seems to be about survival and the faith that you instinctively place in those closest around you. As the circle of trust widens, a new world opens. It is a world with an ever widening set of experiences, that is met with more mystery, and self-discovery within the given boundaries that take place. Cause and effect are the dominant rule going on. I cry and I get fed, cuddled, talked to, given warmth and attention, and so on. Discovery of a burgeoning world. Growth. Moving through the developmental stages, as one new experience is replaced with another. New understandings emerge. Pure innocence in accepting the natural and built world, as I begin to see and frame my life.

Basic attachment principles and survival mechanisms were seemingly fathomless. The bonds that I had with my parent/parents, guardians, close relatives and family friends were the beginnings of the wonderful yet daunting spell through which I undertook life's learning. Those foundational relationships were where I formed and oriented myself to my own set of beliefs, values and a sense of belonging. Initially, I saw the world through my carers' eyes, then began to navigate my own course. As most of us do, I believe.

Following the infant years, the teen years followed with deeper spiritual questions. If there is a God, what is that to me? Growing up in the late sixties, early seventies and eighties, there was much social change and wonderment.

Hold on now. I metaphorically pull the Holden over and park. At this point in the story (surf safari trip), I need to lighten up. Take it all in for a moment. We have been travelling in the Woody for many kilometres. On such a beautiful day, a stop is needed. After all: "Take a break every two hours," right? So, I change pace, and hit the waves. Beautiful. A Slurpee is to follow hopefully. I have spotted a beach break. Perfect three-to-four-foot waves with an off-shore wind blowing. Beautiful faces. So clean. This is worth pulling on the boardies, grabbing the board and paddling out for a surf. When you surf often, you concentrate on only one thing: catching the perfect wave.

My earliest memories of going to the beach are splashing around in the shallows of Chinamans Beach, located in Middle Harbor, Sydney. I am reminded by the family photo album of these experiences. I loved summer and happy playing in the sun and sand. In my primary years, we frequented Freshwater Beach on the Northern Beaches, a contained popular surf beach. There was always a Surf Life Saving patrol on guard: the iconic red and yellow flags pointing to "the safe zone." In the primary years, the summer Saturday morning activity commenced with an early start. Mum never would dilly dally! Arriving in the streets of Freshwater, obtaining a park without too much of a walk, we would descend onto the cool sand and prepare for two hours of extreme fun.

A ritual performed every session was the application of the zinc cream. The bronze zinc cream would be squeezed onto Mum's finger, and then she would smear it all over our nose and cheeks. I cringed at the process, but no one left her tiny beach umbrella without enduring the initiation and almost tribal-like process. Once in the breaking waves, my brother and I, and a random ring-in or two, would splash, kick and paddle our arms in desperate attempts to catch the white, foaming, salty water to the shore. The picture of fervent turtles trying to escape from the clutches of a restricting net. We were lost in the moment of surfing the waves. We held on tight to our red and blue rubber vinyl surf mats. Back in the day, these were the most popular surf craft for kids. They were like a blow-up mattress, only shorter. They had rope handles stitched into the front to grab hold. If you were lucky enough to own a deluxe model, the rubber handles were glued on top, and rubber fins underneath would provide you with superior handling and performance on the waves.

We learnt a lot over the years of summers experienced at the beach. In the early years, it was purely about getting wet and having loads of fun. As we progressed with our surf knowledge and skills of reading the conditions, we became more confident, and would float out the back to attempt catching green waves. A green wave is an unbroken wave. Catching these took way more skill and positioning. A green wave, once on it, enabled you to practice manoeuvring across the face of the wave with speed, ensuring a long ride, until it would eventually break closer to shore. Reading the conditions, like learning to identify rips, gutters and sandbanks, were all part of our beach going education. We truly loved the endless sessions in the waves.

Then we would see her, arm stretched out waving. Our fun was due to come to a close, as the fervent arm waving signalled us to return to the beach. Mum was not someone to take kindly to waiting. With reluctant expressions on our faces, we aimed to catch one more beauty to the shoreline.

Having enjoyed ourselves fully, we returned to the beach beaming with smiles, the zinc cream now a faded smear across our cheeks.

As we packed up, Mum would allow us to buy a lemonade ice-pole from the beach tuck shop. At 11am, as the sand was hotting up, we hopped and skip-ran back to the Kingswood, ready for our return trip home. The trip home was still as much fun, playing corners on the back seat. We slid on the vinyl back bench seat from side to side, bashing then wedging each other firm into the passenger side door. No seat belts in those days to restrain us

As I learnt from a youngster, surfing takes concentration, focus and attention. But sitting out the back of the waves, in between sets, there is time to reflect on all things. The beauty that is surrounding you at that moment—the clear water, the warm sun, magic views, and the waves—is a serene experience. Too often my mind would wander as I went with the flow. Many things entered my mind, and then drifted out of thinking range. It was not an environment where I could remain angry or tense for long. I was soothed by giving over to the elements. Things that needed to be resolved were done so peacefully. Following a surfing session in later years, I would pull out my journal and write with more clarity. It was a place where I could sort out my thinking more coherently. It was private, and my own personal space, not reliant on anyone else. I had found the power of writing.

I was born in 1968, in affluent Sydney, Australia. I grew up in a household registering high levels of testosterone with a matriarch who ruled the roost ferociously. But it was "Absolutely Fabulous." I remember enjoying the series of this sitcom through my primary and teen years. A unique and quirky family mix was the appeal. Quite unlike ours. Though the lead character reminded me of my own mum in a strange way. The co-star on the show shared a relationship much like the one my mother had with my godmother. The expression "Absolutely Fabulous" sums things up regarding our home life. I make a point of stating this in a positive light at this part of the journey.

Our transition was not the easiest though, and complicated for a period. It was a time of confusion for my older brothers, then for myself and my baby brother. Mum was at her most vulnerable during the immediate time following Dad's death. We grieved over the death of my father for quite a time. A total shock for any partner to experience so young in a relationship. There were many months where, as a family, we relied on our extended family and friends to survive.

Mum had an enormous job on her hands, which was to rear four infant boys. It would have been a terrible time navigating our future while carrying her grief and realising the job of caring for her young family solo. Confusion.

Pain. An overwhelming numbness too. I query whether Mum's needs were ever met. After some time, she just got on with the job of being a single parent.

Due to the support of a nurse friend of the family following Dad's death, we were destined to a place where we could join in a wonderful neighbourhood community, where many positive memories were forged. This was the home where most of my memories were made within our family unit. We were forged together as a strong family unit from a very early stage of life. There is more to the story here, however details are not needed. Mum eventually sold the Killara home.

Before I share my overall positive experiences, I need to write about a time though that was by no means fabulous. I'd like to just get it out of the way at this part of my story. There was a short period in my childhood years when my family home was a foreign place to me. It was not such a favourite place of mine. I do remember some of Mum's male friends who entered my childhood, and we did have an association with the group Parents Without Partners for a period. My memories of this period were of gatherings, such as picnics, and activities with other single parent families. Relationships for Mum must have been challenging as she focused on her job as provider for her four sons. After some time, Mum remarried for a period of less than two years. Then divorced. It was an ugly divorce too. So the details are not necessary for the purposes here. Let's just say I do believe that period affected me, and my emotional wellbeing.

Overall, though, home was a great place to be. I hope the other family members concur with this overall perspective.

In coping with the loss of Dad... I was so young. But. It must have imprinted itself indelibly on my development. I was just too young to know. In my primary years, trying to understand Mum's decision to find a partner was so difficult. I had a hard time replacing one father with now a stepfather. What could an eleven-year-old do? The two years that this man was in our lives was marked with another life change for me: I quit my rugby union team to play soccer. Soccer was the passion for this man. Rugby wasn't supported. After his removal and the subsequent divorce, I returned to footy where my true passion lay. My beloved game and team.

Thoughts, ideas, learning to love, values and life perspectives were developing within this new context. During the early infant days, months and years at our humble abode, I began carving the little individual I was to become. I was lucky. It was within the loving confines of my family home that I naturally began to be me. For the most part this was in St Ives. Each of my brothers and I eventually flew the coop from that humble abode.

Our life was never dull. It was packed full of energy, activities and people visiting associated with many aspects of our colourful lives. It was an exciting childhood: busy and never dull. Beyond the faded white and chipped timber framed windows, and behind our distinctive red brick and heavy grey terracotta tiled roof, was a world of all sorts of misadventures for the Bennett boys. We had plenty of space in our quarter-acre level block: a big grassy backyard for playing footy, soccer, cricket, and for riding our BMX bikes in laps around the edges of the yard. Later, a half-sunken in-ground vinyl pool was added.

The pets were precious, and we always had a dog. A Boxer-cross-Labrador named Major, picked and named by Stuart, my brother: short-haired tan and white in colour, a lovable and friendly dog. He featured the sleek and muscular body of the Boxer breed, with the friendly face of a Labrador. He would always sit on your foot when resting inside. We were informed this was an odd characteristic of Boxers. His early death of heartworm, which he contracted from another neighbourhood dog, was devastating.

Curie featured for a couple of years: a Kelpie with boundless energy, another rescue dog named after the well-known scientist Marie Curie. My memories of this dog are blanked out. I believe my time was spent away from our home and backyard as much as possible, at age eleven and twelve, for reasons mentioned above. I chose to remove myself from the strange, adult male figure who occupied our once happy and safe play space.

Then there was Tim, who was a non-stop go get- 'em black Kelpie. Chosen and adored by Andrew, he was a much-loved family friend. He was a dog of healing, and my attachment with him lasted into my late teens. Suburban life in the end became too frustrating for him. He used to trot around the edges of our metal-capped pool, snapping at flies with his jaws. He was destined for our uncle and aunt's farm and found his calling as a snake dog there. A worthy role.

Then a cat was thrown into our household for those years the intruder lived under our roof. I named her Mischief. But she only responded to Puss.

My final pet was a bird. Olly. I was fortunate to be part of a joint project with my eldest brother John constructing an aviary. As an experiment, I bred the peach face parrots for a short while too.

When my parents were first married, Mum (Jan) and Dad (Frank), owned their house in Killara, another suburb of Sydney's northern region. This home carries many deeply rooted memories. Most of them I am not able to retrieve for being so young. I have many photographs kept in the family album to remind me of such times. I reflect on what happy times they must have been, going on the expressions of the faces captured in those photos. Different family members feature in a range of events and activities.

As a middle child with three brothers, I think I did

influence the family with my coming into the world. Even if, in later years, it was seen to be a bumpy ride. My aunts, particularly though, have reminded me along the way that I was a content and happy baby, the joy of my father's attention. He too was a middle child of four boys. I was lucky to have a unique bond with Frank, as my two older brothers, John at seven and Stuart at five, were experiencing a different relationship with Mum and Dad. The gap in developmental years, I believe, meant a significant difference in my relationship and attachment at this stage of life.

About Dad's death.

Mum received a call one afternoon. Frank had experienced a heart attack. That afternoon, he had been playing his favourite game of lawn bowls. He still hadn't returned home when the family doctor called mum. Dad was bought back to our house and, due to the lack of medical intervention at the time, died the same day. At age forty-one. For my mother, the loss, grief and pain of my dad's death was crushing. Mum stated in later life on many occasions that she thought that she and Dad would be like a Darby and Joan couple. I guess by this she meant that they would have lived a happy and loving long life together. A pigeon pair. Living with this broken dream must have been incomprehensible.

Reflecting on things for the greater period of my life, I

can see that my three brothers and I all share one common thing. It is the fact of not having a dad growing up that has bound us. Dad's death, in the year of 1969, has had ramifications for each of us in turn, that have shaped each one of us to the very core, I believe. Talk about initiation, this would prove to be one of life's biggies in my book. And I am not alone in thinking this way. The celebration of Father's Day for my dad has been missing in my calendar lifelong. The immediate days following were a shocking reality for everyone. The ramifications of the death of our primary bread winner, loving husband, colleague, brother, friend, son, and father, was almost too big to process.

My mother, brothers and I were to be caught up in the turmoil of things. In the short, medium and long term, our lives were turned upside down. Our family environment was never to be "the norm." All of us were now impacted by the influence of those around us, more than ever. We would be for life, really. Such a turn of events brought our family unit very close, and every relationship was impacted. All the tremendous effort from our extended family members were at force. Nanna and Pa, Pop and Nan, Mum's sisters' families, the Bradleys, the Bennetts, and Helen.

Dad was a journalist with the Australian Broadcasting Commission. From letters we received from all over the country at the time of Dad's death, he was an admired and well-respected professional within the media. Reading those letters in recent years has led me to understand the added weight of my dad's death on Mum. She was the partner of a well-known public figure, making Dad's death more difficult. The nation joined in the mourning and loss of a warm individual. Frank Bennett.

I had experienced much unconscious attachment and strong bonds within my family unit prior to Dad's death. Mum, Dad, two older brothers and a loving extended family. A normal nuclear family. The deep loss of my dad would leave a stain on my psyche for life, a clear chink in the armour of my life. This was to be now an abnormal family life experience. In all of our lives, we experienced this tragedy the same way, differently, altogether, and separately. Added to the situation was the fact that Mum was pregnant with my younger brother. He was to be born completely into a fatherless existence only months later that same year. We were to be a family of four boys, and a mum.

5
My Spirit Beckons: Good Timing and Safe Taming

From infancy I was destined to be an optimist. Despite the early blows that life threw at me and my family, I just seemed to get on with things. Essentially, I was happy. Loved. I always had all that I really needed. I had a firm attachment within my family.

Jumping ahead for a moment, it was in my mid-teens that I latched on to the Bible verse: "All things work together for good, for those who love God," Romans 8:28. I learnt to have determination from a young age. I built in a sense of remaining positive. I still believe in the power of this verse. My mother, who passed on 10 August 2015, would be happy to hear me quote this, as she was the one who shared it with me first. She was responsible for my initial awareness of the importance of having spirituality in my life. It must have guided her too during troubled times.

My worries did come, but not till later. I'll explain this further down the track. The lessons of life are often hard and can bring about pivotal moments of profound change that remain embedded in the fabric of one's life. Those lessons have each, in turn, made me. Either way, there is an old saying: "What doesn't kill you makes you stronger." But, in my experience, that is much easier said than lived.

This chapter is about my 'response to responsibility.' I explore this subject area more in detail later, as I begin orienting my chapters in the book around themes relating to the developmental happenings of that particular age. I can more accurately describe my experiences not only from my own memory bank, but in parallel with observing the development of my two sons.

Life at five years young. Sport always featured in the Bennett household. I followed on the heels of my two older brothers in many sporting adventures. They opened all sorts of learning and development, and a variety of activities were available to choose from.

Let me turn off the freeway in my Kingswood, pull over metaphorically, and take another break from things. I will just chill out for a bit, and reflect on some sporting endeavours, as I survey the break in front of me. What were the good times?

On a Saturday morning session, during the winter months, my mother frequently took my younger brother and me to several ice rinks in the Sydney area. This weekend activity encompassed much physical development, as we curved around corner after corner, lap after lap, in a bid to experience the wind across the face in a gliding sensation with little effort. It was the need for speed that did it every time. I was well coordinated, and so most sports came naturally. Mum gave us this great opportunity to perform in an environment where we could really live it up.

My brother and I were free to be budding speed skaters, mixing it with the locals and other kids who were testing their abilities on the ice. Being a kid on an outing with your mum is fine at five and six, and seven. I was not quite at the stage of being too cool to let it worry me. I can remember liking the fact that Mum was around; we had someone to demonstrate our abilities to, to show off to. My younger brother and I, and often one of our school friends as a tag along, enjoyed the two or three-hour session as time was suspended. We were totally in the moment. Bliss.

The freedom really began when I left the area where we laced up in the ice-skating boots. We still relied on Mum to make sure the laces were tight. We sought to avoid any potential sprains of ankles, or loss of skating form. And then we entered the arena full of excitement and nervous confidence. Clutching the barrier for the first few meters to find our feet, then letting go. We were off, and on our own, for as long as we could stand the pain in our feet. It was always a challenge to see who held out the longest before retiring back to the seated area for a break.

This initial rush the ice rink, I'm sure, lasted for longer and longer over the season, as we would inevitably become accustomed to the torture and pain in our feet and shins. I can recall even using a little tool that my other brothers had dispensed with which helped you ensure that the laces were able to be pulled so tight it could have been comparable to torture.

As my older brothers considered themselves the big boys, the days of needing assistance in most sporting pursuits were gone. The little ice-skating tool became a prized possession. It made me feel special since I rarely saw anybody else use one. As nearly all my skating experiences were without my older brothers, this activity was new and exciting. It was not a hand-me down activity, as so many were. By obtaining the little tool we were following in others' footsteps. In this case, a sliding kind of style move. The pain of wearing the boots was a small price to pay for the freedom and self-expression that was mine in the arena, sliding around without a care for hours.

One particular lesson I learnt the hard way. My mother never forgot it either, as we chuckled about it as adults, years later. We visited one of the rinks located on the Northern Beaches peninsular at Narrabeen. We arrived for our standard ice-skating session of fun on a rainy day in winter. My younger brother and I were around six and seven, and quite able on the ice. Each of us had reasonable confidence and capability, even though we were young.

The physical dimensions of this rink were notable. It was smaller than other rinks. The fact is though, it was a small rink compared to other venues like Prince Alfred in the city, or Canterbury Ice Rink. The other problem was that the ice at one end had worn to a corrugated finish, much like a panel of roofing iron, and would give you the wobbles each time you skated around that corner section. It was this section that indeed made the rink unique. It caused much grief during each session. Once we navigated it for the first dozen times, we did get used to it. It would slow people down a little as they negotiated their moves to get around it before proceeding to head back in the other direction.

One day, I was merrily skating along, enjoying my freedom and drifting around with my mind in my own little world, when suddenly, as I've come around the corrugated section with relative ease, I straightened, picking up more speed into the straight. I dodged a couple of slower moving skaters, and then a very large woman just ahead of me made an awkward attempt to make a nervous dash into the middle of the rink. In an instant, I collided with her, bounced off her, fell and smacked my head upon the surface of the ice. I was knocked out cold, and the only thing I remember after that was waking up sitting on Mum's lap, sucking a redskin lollipop. I cannot recall skating at that rink again. It did not stop me from skating over the following months and years at other rinks. I still had many other positive experiences and recall the fun times with my family, youth groups and other friends into my teens.

My skating freedom and greater self-awareness demonstrated in small ways that I was beginning to understand my part in accepting greater responsibility for my own actions. I could no longer hide behind my role in the ice-skating incident. In everyday life I was learning that my actions had consequences. From this life stage, I began mixing it up in a bigger world circle than ever before.

Accepting the harsh consequences of the "bigger world" was partially met with reluctance. Who wants to grow up? Peter Pan had a life outlook and approach to the subject of childhood that most kids would have aspired to. An enticing wonderment and anticipation of what might be next was always present in my developing five-, six-, and seven-year-old mind and heart. I remember the revelation when I realised that my pants had become ankle freezers—short longs, or long shorts.

In my old house, it was a real treat to have Mum open the camphorwood chest and bring out these mothballs-smelling, neatly folded t-shirts and pants. They were hand me downs from older brothers and cousins. And some of the items were real rippers: one of the benefits of older brothers and cousins. It was a Christmas treat in September. The call to responsibility was fast knocking at the door of my cubby-house-framed world. Some housekeeping rules were needing to be laid down. In our family home, and all around in different places, there were tough guidelines. Some of the rules were very unpopular at the time but would prove to be invaluable later.

As I continued exploring new areas of my life, I experienced many first-time events and situations which were presenting themselves, as they do in the expanding world of a youngster. There was a certain requirement to step up and respond responsibly in many new areas of my life. This rapid realisation hit me as I commenced school, and was also a part of the new rules of sports. Organised sports and activities are another complete dimension of a kid's world of new learnings and life experiences.

Suddenly, my social world was expanding at an increasing rate and the inevitability of new-found events and experiences commanded much more of me than I first imagined. Life became busier with the onset of these many new experiences. Part and parcel of growing up really. For me at this stage, it all seemed good. But looking back and recording them in this book, perhaps they were not such an easy thing to deal with. As a kid, my life was about change. I was just going with it all. I did not see any dramas on the horizon.

Maybe I needed a more flexible approach to life, to its pressing rules and impending change. Just as I experienced the world of gymnastics at a tender age, I sought to become flexible. The challenges of gymnastics laid the steppingstones for the onset of my early teens and expanding social world. My mother's parenting and firm decision-making, although often perceived by me as harsh, stood me in good stead. I have carried many of these parenting qualities into my own child rearing.

Learning these life lessons was a real trial, but the world of gymnastics opened a new door. I assume that most of you are familiar with gymnastics. It takes dedication and practice to get high level results within the discipline. The expectation was not to end up as a first-rate gymnast. It was about taking responsibility to see a commitment through within the activity. By expressing an interest and enthusiasm in doing it, I made a commitment to seeing through a full term in view of the fees paid by my mother.

The scene was set at our local community YMCA. I remember walking through the double glass doors and being immediately confronted with kids running, jumping, bouncing, rolling and flexing themselves, all dressed in their white shorts and t-shirts. All activities were performed in bare feet, however the noises that could be heard were thumping on mats, slight creaking of equipment, chattering, and small-voiced shouting of excitement from the budding gymnasts themselves. Over this were the voices of various instructors, belting out a command for a certain manoeuvre to be attempted and repeated. Energy abounded in the hall, coupled with an atmosphere full of electric motion and movement, buzzing energy on display.

The lesson was that my mother was not going to let me pass this opportunity up too easily. I was initially overwhelmed by the environment in which this activity of gymnastics took place. It was strange to me how the children were organised in groups to perform what seemed like a version of recruitment for the circus. After my early reservations, due to the cost of the fees and the commitment I had made to my mother, I saw the term through. I was to come every Tuesday to the class and did not dare argue with my mother who would brook no resistance. I remember putting on a show, and protesting the situation, but there was no avoiding completing the term with my mum.

Looking back, with four boys to look after, fees to be outlaid and times to be organised for activities, it would have been a difficult thing to juggle for all of us. It was difficult not having a spouse to support Mum, and not having someone to assist with the financial and emotional support or having help disciplining four children. As a little boy, I was not aware of the difficulty of the money side of things as I was largely shielded.

I did enjoy the commitment to gymnastics in the long run and developed many skills and flexibility in physical terms. Lifelong learning came later as a result of following through, due to Mum's quality parenting. My association with gymnastics would eventually be quite rewarding. I did go on to become a casual gymnastics instructor after high school two days a week at the same YMCA. It was my first steady employment as a teenager.

The learning of responsibility came in various ways. I thought it was one of those things that you can choose to accept or not. In reality, I am not sure there really is a choice. It either comes gradually or smacks you hard.

Both forms of learning responsibility impacted on me through primary, high school, and beyond. Sometimes a breeze, other times quite painful. In my younger years, most of the lessons were wrapped up with care, not cotton wool. Support that allowed self-learning and personal confidence to grow and develop at my own pace. I became my own judge.

Within the context of gymnastics, the trampoline was one of my most loved pieces of equipment. The art of bouncing and performing manoeuvres in free flight was pure fun and I loved the sense of freedom. The parallel bars enabled the beginnings of upper body development. Strength and endurance, which I took with me into the sport of surfing.

Talking about surfing. Enough pondering. Out into the surf break I will go. Handbrake on. Check. Windows up. Check. Boardies on, rashie too. Waxing of board. Off I go, to be back in a couple of hours refreshed. Oh yeah. Nearly forgot the tribal application of the zinc cream. Thanks, Mum.

Mum and Dad

Dad and baby Mitch, 1968

On the farm, 1972

Rabbiting at the farm, 1972

Feeding cows, 1972

Bennett boys, 1973

Family photo, 1979

House Captain Year 6, 1980

BMX mud, 1973

Geroa, 7 Mile Beach

Mini-bike riding, 1980

Skateboarding, 1984

Surf trip, 1987

Andy surfing, 1988

Windsurfing, 1990

Family photo, 1991

6
A Vigorous All-Rounder: Rough and Ready to Play

Innocence surrounded my childhood experiences for the most part. However, childhood comes and goes. Where and when did I cross the line? It was soon an emerging realisation that I played a real part in my own destiny. Those emerging scary moments in which I found myself moving more into a world of greater awareness, where I was less blinkered, slowly became more frequent. In many ways, I interpreted the signs that life was a race. It was not just my perception. I needed to compete to survive, achieving in a range of life areas as I went. A fierce awakening.

I was waking up to the realities of life. My childhood amnesia was not a dream state any longer. There was a real world turning, and I was part of the events occurring all around. I questioned myself, wondering if I gained an awareness of things too early. Was this a boy thing, or the competitiveness of living in a household of three other males? But it came from other avenues as well.

An example comes to mind. As an early awakening, it was harmless. Yet on the other hand, it led to a significant leap forward in my own development as a young boy who had influence. Following on from my five- and six-year-old days, and now moving into my seventh, and eighth years of boyhood, I explore this next stage.

I joined the Boy Cub's movement early. It was a membership where I gained a great deal of learning and experienced much fun. Its motto was: "Be prepared." I had many adventures, and gained a broad range of practical skills, as well as deep friendships made in the weekly meetings. I participated in outings and camps, canoeing, sailing, hiking and weekly meetings. I grew accustomed to the routine and learnt of the principles of giving back to the community responsibly. I have carried this learning into my adult years, and now find myself passing it on to my own two boys.

A new stage dawned: Scouts. I now faced a process of leaping forward, having completed this childhood stage. There were some friends that accompanied me on this next part of the journey, but there was anxiety in leaving the group I knew. What was this new realm going to offer? I wondered. My pathway was set, like my two older brothers who had previously made the leap some years back. I aspired to follow the trail they had followed. I do not remember having a conversation about this initiation process with either of my brothers. It was a new experience.

There were many appealing aspects to joining the Scouts. I would be able to wear a fully brimmed, pressed felt hat, and have the opportunity to achieve the status of an Assistant Patrol Leader (APL), or even Patrol Leader (PL). This meant I could be able to proudly wear their badge and cord upon my uniform. Both roles were distinguished positions, especially to a "grub," oops, I mean cub. The badges they attained for different kinds of services to the community or developing skills were way cool too.

If I am honest, it didn't take long to be convinced that this step into Scouts was the right one. Extra responsibility brought excitement with it. I contemplated the status of being adopted as one of the "louts," oh, I mean scouts! There was some change in the uniform, and the hat was a significant indicator of more importance and a higher level of status. My time to jump the rope had come upon me. This memory was important, as that "leaping forward" in the seventies and eighties occurred in every Cub and Scout troop across all regions. The discovery of young manhood was emerging within this association.

The act of jumping over the rope was highly symbolic. Two scouts held a rope with some slack along a marked line about three meters long. The idea was to jump the rope with one big stride over to the other side, thus signifying the crossing over and upwards into this new realm and movement of Scouts. What was unexpected though was the elected scouts at either end holding the rope would flick it taut. It should have been a simple leap over the relaxed rope to the other side, as if crossing the divide. This simple test tricked the first couple of eager beaver cubs. Those who followed in the ceremony soon wised up. Crossing the great divide and entering "lout-hood," or Scouts, provided the first of many initiation encounters we would be subject to.

Fairly harmless really. It was not that big a deal, but it marked an important stage of surprise, and the new adventures ahead. Learning how to function in a microcosm society as young people, we developed through a safe and mature context of informal and formal lessons, wrapped in fun. I continued with Scouts for a few years, also experiencing another troop that my brothers were not part of. I migrated to this group as they were closer to home, and I had formed close friendships with a couple of high school mates who attended this group. Peer influence was always a factor growing up.

The initiation process would prove to be a reoccurring theme. Many of the range of safe activities and learning during these developmental years were framed with the theme of transitioning from boyhood to manhood. We may not have known exactly what we were being prepared for, but education was very popular during these times, with a rich tradition and history. In our society, initiation processes, however subtle, are an inevitable deal of growing up. Teens were tempting, and the lure of what was next was something to ponder. The growing magnetism to hungrily seeking out what was ahead was powerful. I was satisfied, but the pressure to be something more was apparent.

On the theme of "being prepared": as cubs and scouts, we were taught to keep ten cents tucked within our safety wallet for emergencies. Soon it went to twenty cents. The price of a public phone call doubled, it seemed, overnight. Today, I still like to keep a ten or twenty dollar note in my wallet, for any unexpected reason. Those unexpected events still crop up in life. The lessons I learned in Cubs I can still appreciate in today's world. Today, my youngest son would reply with: "All you need is your mobile phone, Dad."

I have read a few books around the growing of boys to men. To help me in my masculinity, and the shaping of my fatherhood, this has been beneficial. The idea of initiation within a couple of these publications, have challenged my thinking on the subject. My own take on this one sits differently with some of the views in "boys to men" publications. My own take and experience on the subject are a melting pot of many philosophies. I have taken the learning traits of parenting from many sources really. If I was a chef, I would look at parenting as requiring many ingredients to produce that special meal. Parenting requires many good additives to achieve a well-rounded individual.

I think I have been able to apply the right mixture to the process of growing our two boys. The books on what constitutes real masculinity have been very informative. I have observed all types of men my whole life, sometimes quite critically. I bring it all to my parenting. Instead of seeing things through an "initiation lens," I have preferred the act of providing, where I could, a considered "first-time experience" in their lives. Life is full of firsts. And this time, I do not mean in a competition sense.

As I wrote this, I shared the experiences outlined above with my child. As an eight-year-old, I have no doubt that self-determination was alive and kicking in me as a child. When my son is old enough to want to plough through this book, he may well be reminded of some of the "firsts" lessons learned during this stage of discovery, as well as understanding the possibilities that lay ahead, and the inbuilt pressure of exposure to new experiences. All areas of life are susceptible to learning about difficulties and joys.

Those influential years of growth and development are fully loaded years. A "firecracker" experience could have wonderful and beautiful end effects or could, in some cases, lead to disaster, and outcomes scarring one for a lifetime. But learning is learning. And the life lessons are there for the experiencing. I remember reading a book some many years ago, which promoted the notion that we indeed place our own lessons before us.

I return in my thoughts to primary school. The nine o'clock bell has been rung, the Australian flag raised, and I am about to start school for the day. My primary school years began in the 1970s. No such thing as the Aboriginal and Torres Strait Islander flags flying alongside the Australian flag then. However, I'm glad to say that my children's education has been truly complimented by having Indigenous studies within their curriculum. And the Aboriginal and Torres Strait Islander flags have flown alongside the Australian flags from their first days of school. Changes are apparent, it would seem.

I start with the lessons learned in the sporting context. Even with my pre-existing sporting ability, attempting to clear hurdles on athletics track during these years was not an easy task. My legs just were not that long at that age. I was of primary school age and small in relative terms. I would have preferred age-appropriate size hurdles, but no such things existed. I greatly desired small life lessons that were easy to digest, not these big life lessons. What are the expectations put before primary-aged children? At times, are the lessons too big, or too challenging? I explore further.

I was big framed, and simply not that fast a runner. My

domain was not track and field, except the one true race of choice. I still claim to be a real winner at this activity: the three-legged race. My school mate and I achieved amazing status due to the three-legged race notoriety for several years in those school carnival events. Partnered with a mate of similar track and field ability, bound by a nylon stocking around our left and right ankle, there was no stopping us. We would canter in unison down the track to an unbeatable victory every time.

The results in this area of sporting achievements, coupled with a few other abilities, forged much competence and confidence in other quirky races. The sack race, and egg-and-spoon race, where I gained a personal best, taught that this period of life was more about being wrapped up in having fun, rather than focusing on a hard-core, driven competitive pursuit. Or being driven to conquer any such hard life lessons. I liked it this way.

Tony (my victory-bound mate) and I took the three-legged race seriously on those occasions that we were put to the test, I can tell you. The foundational platform for life that was firming up may just have been the lesson that simply participating was a key. And not just that but enjoying the event with a mate. Particularly as we were prone to having a scrap with each other before the track and field activities as a team. All I can say now is, Tony, thanks for allowing me as a left footer to do my thing.

When thinking about primary school, there is a standout memory at eight years of age. It is a negative memory, as I was given no choice but to repeat Year Two. There is a lot of stigma attached, in those days at least. On the plus side, the attachment second time around to my teacher Mrs. Evans and her teaching style in this year was all important. She was a gently spoken and a considered woman, though vibrant and fun too. And attractive and kind. My Year Two second time round was a winner year. But it did put me behind my peers, however, for some time to come.

The receiving of merit awards for written expression in my work later in Years Three and Four stood out as positive reinforcement of my intellectual worth. School life did improve, countering the negative situation of repeating. I was glad to have the hard evidence to prove that I did well in those later years. My mother kept several of the merit awards for many years, and later, they were shown to me, along with my track and field ribbons. Parents can be so embarrassing, and yet so cool.

This is something that I have done with my own children, keeping their achievement awards from school and other areas in a safe place. Not to be embarrassing of course. The retention of awards and confirmation of achievements during those influential years is important for the sound development of a child. Otherwise, without confirmation and praise, a child could be left wondering how they measure up against their peers. The inevitability of peer pressure was something that we all endured. The social world of the institutional school environment is certainly a testing ground of things to come in later life.

School was certainly compulsory in New South Wales. I was very fortunate to experience learning in a "rich learning" environment. I was required to attend whether I liked it or not. I can remember crying on my first day. The local primary school was the beginnings of many good things to come, and its motto "Learn to Live," the script on our school shield emblem, still impresses me today as a simple, but profound, statement.

Respect for authority was a good thing in my case and abiding by the rules kept me on the straight and narrow. Discipline and the routine of school was important, as I did have a scallywag element in my behaviour. My relationship with my head mistress/principal, Miss Cassidy, was one of fond association and mutual respect. Although, one of my schoolboy stunts resulted in me being under the spotlight for some time after.

As a result of the time spent with Miss Cassidy, there was many a positive exchange and correction of my behaviour over a variety of issues. I never saw the cane though, as it was not a form of discipline used at our school in the years I attended. The principal was as much a part of the surrounds as the chalk boards and dusters. There were always boxes of chalk and chalk dust floating around, finding rest on every ledge. Miss Cassidy would float around too, and you never knew where she might appear. She must have had even more special powers of surveillance as head teacher.

As students, we were always reminded while in class that each teacher had eyes in the back of their head. I certainly never wished to be on the receiving end of one of those canes. I did though grow up in an era where the cane apparently could be used. Perhaps the stories were spread from schools in surrounding suburbs, and by those rascal boys at private schools who, in my view, were surely more deserving subjects of this harsh treatment for unruly behaviour.

Many years of solid learning at that school contributed to my later life achievements. They were lessons kindly laid down and have remained important. Without such a stimulating environment packed full of lessons around the various wonders of the world my life would be all the poorer. My later life opportunities were bolstered by these starting blocks. I was able to step up in fine form for the race of life and experience being a humble participant among a fine line up of other small starters.

Many years on I have had the privilege of once again meeting my teacher of the third grade, Mrs. Percy. I have also been able to visit my principal, Miss Cassidy. Upon meeting them, they did not seem that different. In appearance and character! Maybe teachers do carry some status of immortality. I must confess that I now understand home and school whisperings much more so as a parent myself. I am aware that a child's voice needs always to be listened to and not just heard, by their mum, dad, grandparents, carers, aunts and uncles, and guardians and carers/friends alike to whom they trust. It is a reciprocal act of love and necessary for the survival of us all.

7
Begone My Mind Adrift …
Begin the Forming of My Faith

What has interested me in my adult years, and as I have written this book, is the power of memory. I have been blessed or cursed with a pretty good memory. Everyone reading this book no doubt has memories that have travelled with them, of all sorts of events. As children especially, these memories are all important. We are like sponges, and impressionable. When there are the hard things we remember, we can also draw upon good memories. Memories, good or bad, stack up through a layering process. They can be powerful, influential, throughout our lives, and long lasting. Our subconscious is powerful, as we try to fathom the memories on a deeper level. Our recollections also play a part in changing the course of direction for us.

Only I can ultimately weigh up the role certain memories played in my developing years, or how they have served me in later years. I have been ably assisted by the help of others to reflect on moments throughout life. I am highlighting that memories are powerful though. As our thoughts stack up, they create depth, and experiences gain a history. Negative memories can, though, be replaced with more powerful positive memories. Time may bring healing, but it often requires work to come through.

With the skills of a good guide, the layering can become more solid and convert to a stable structure. Seek out people gifted and trained to help healing occur around memories and trauma. Friendships can also serve as powerful support.

A prominent figure for me as a young person was a superhero named Astro Boy, a fictional cartoon character robot created by a Dr Elephant. I related strongly to Astro Boy as a child. He was pint sized when we were introduced, like me. His focus was to participate in adventures to rescue others, and fight for justice. I felt I too was made of tough stuff, but with a soft heart. Not exactly like Astro Boy. Who was half-human half-robot. Though Astro Boy also had a sensitive side to him. He also questioned things a lot.

I thought I was expected to be tough enough to take on life's challenges. As I aspired to such a superhero, I realised I was subject to vulnerabilities. And maybe not so tough in some ways. Memories from my childhood have in small ways created a "chink in the armour." Other life experiences have fatigued me deeply and penetrated to the core of my humanness. I have had various welders who came to my rescue and, over time, patched up the exposed wounds needing attention.

Each of my "fixer-up people" helped me reframe the vision needed to restore me to wholeness again. Most importantly they allowed me to re-create myself. They had a role similar to an alchemist. Noun: tempering. The degree of hardiness and elasticity in steel or other metal. Verb: improve the hardiness and elasticity of (steel or other metal) by reheating and then cooling it.

For children, the role of a parent or care giver is to bring guidance, with attributes including sensitivity, perception and intuition, skilfully wrapped in love. For the child, a gentle tempering process takes place. Creating safe environments, not totally risk free though, for children is paramount for solid construction of the "stuff of us." If we are fortunate to have loving, supportive adults and seniors care for us, we certainly have a head start. I had such a beginning, as I grew from infancy to my teens. I was made vulnerable by Dad's death as an infant, and Mum's remarrying and divorce as a young primary-aged child. But I received much love and kindness from relatives and friends. This went to balancing out things.

A little more on tempering. Adjective: good-tempered. A good-tempered person or animal is naturally friendly and pleasant and does not easily get angry or upset. She/he was a happy, good-tempered child. I have observed tempering in all families. I have seen it in a loving context. Minimising harm, both emotional and physical. I have witnessed tempering, or forms of harsh discipline administered without love, affecting individuals and families negatively. Abuse is never tempering.

Emotional and physical abuse can affect all types of behaviour in response. Different paths of behaviour may create unsteady platforms for a child to build their life upon. This is a child at risk. In my later studies in social work, psychologist Eric Erickson began an understanding of how and where the foundations for youth need to be formed. A solid framework is based on firm foundational footings. Like a house, having solid emotional footings provides the platform from where we begin to work out basic belief systems and values, along with other psychological necessities which equip us for the survival of each chapter in life.

In my own childhood, I have wondered if the subconscious burying of emotion was born due to such deep separation from my father. I missed out on important initiation processes growing up with Dad. I sometimes competed so hard with myself and was accustomed to almost beating myself up. I ended up excelling in almost all areas that I engaged in as a child and adolescent. Except, I lacked concentration within the classroom environment, and my schoolwork suffered. I fell behind through primary school, and this followed me in the high school years.

Ironically, I am writing this early in the morning, as I celebrate Father's Day. I am reminded of not being able to celebrate Father's Day with my own dad. Thankfully I celebrate this event every year now, with a Happy Father's Day. As a dad. The good outweighs the bad. The memories of loss from not being able to celebrate with my dad, I have replaced with good memories of joy. And I have now let go of such emotions as sorrow and anger over the event of his death. An event I had no control over. I can and do now breathe much more easily! The weight of sorrow has been lifted.

Forging our identity happens from the word go. The "chipping away" process of modelling our personalities helps fashion the very individuals we are. Like in the formation of a sculpture. I have found the years leading up to my adolescence were full of scrapes and bruises of the physical sort, coupled with various emotional challenges. Like the time I was playing one weekend at my local primary school.

The school grounds in those days provided a wonderland of adventure without staff supervision, and well outside the weekly, fixed routine. The routine was replaced by the freedom of timeless fun on a Saturday and Sunday. We would ride our bikes, run around, roller skate and skateboard to our hearts' content. There were so many concreted surfaces to whirl around on. The fields were also kept nicely mown, so kicking the footy and soccer ball around was also a great space to share with other kids from around the neighbourhood.

The outside perimeter of the school fencing was a mere meter high. This section was not cared for, a "no man's land." This strip was just over the other side of the groomed grounds, to the north of the infants' playground. Long weed-like grass and foliage. On this occasion, foolishly in bare feet, I jumped the fence, on my way back to a mate's house. Always in such a rush, I sprinted carefree through the long grass, in full momentum. My next stride fell with a fatal stomp. I buckled as my foot landed on something sharp. I found myself sitting down, clasping my foot, panicking at the amount of blood streaming out of the wound. The pain was unbearable. I suddenly felt sick in the stomach.

After several minutes assessing my gashed foot, and gaining composure, I managed to stand up, and began limping to the closest point of refuge, which was my mate's house over the street, on the corner of the block. Slowly, step by step, only placing the heel of my injured foot on the ground, I painfully made my way to this safe place. This house was a port of call on weekends. As a tribe of kids, we would make raids to various houses usually for food stops and/or a quick dip in someone's pool. Luckily for me, my mate's mum was home.

After such an ordeal, my mum was eventually called, and a doctor's visit occurred shortly after. At the local doctor's surgery, I was ushered straight in to see the doctor. I explained the events that had taken place earlier. My foot was now under examination. Unknowingly, the doctor stitched whatever it was that had caused the gash, into the sole of my foot! Little did I know this was the case. A routine procedure of stitching a gash to the sole of my left foot—not so.

Over time the internal swelling became too uncomfortable to bear. As mums are so good at doing, thorough follow up took place: the foreign body was surgically removed under a general anaesthetic in hospital some months after the incident. What an ordeal that experience was.

My love of skateboarding developed in those school grounds as well. Left foot planted firmly on the deck, right leg striding as I pounded the pavement to gain momentum, the whoosh was so fulfilling. I would speed down the path crouched slightly, swerving and tick-taking to keep the flow. My mates and I visited skate bowls in another suburb close by as the years went by, where we would cruise the ramps all day. These were great memories leading well into my teens!

Meanwhile, back in the school grounds, one of those

endless weekends again, I was sitting on my skateboard deck with linked legs in a catamaran configuration with a mate. My feet on his deck, his on mine, facing each other. We were on a fairly steep section of the path, however we needed to work as a two-person team to steer both skateboards forward, and gain speed. We would lean towards, and away from each other, together, to swerve and enhance the ride. Most often it worked.

This time we did not work in unison. I did not lean enough, and we pulled apart. Our speed meant I experienced the death wobbles. This is when you are travelling so fast that the skateboard begins to perform small radical turns left to right. The wobbles increase in severity, and faster and faster you go before you spin out of control. Predictably, I fell off, scraping my rear on the asphalt for meters, burning a hole through my shorts and ripping layers of skin off. I remember school on Monday, wearing a nappy-like pad to stop the weeping of blood and pus. It stopped the staining of my uniform too. Embarrassing, as you can imagine.

These events are a good indication of my character that was becoming evident during my primary years: daring, adventurous, and a little bit crazy at times, usually in the name of fun. In all things though, I was displaying that I was also resilient. The "chipping away" process, and the tempering by others too, was doing its work, shaping my form in all ways: physically, emotionally, mentally and spiritually.

Briefly now, I re-engage my thinking to the metaphorical surf safari journey I am taking you on. The road trip consists of only four main elements: Number 1. Surfing. Number 2. Sleeping. Number 3. Writing, and Number 4. Eating. The latter usually involves quite a bit of takeaway, as you can imagine. Though if camping was involved, the old gas stove would get a solid work out. I have been known to try and cook an egg, and make coffee at the same time, all on the one burner. Quite an accomplishment.

Like many surf safaris, the local hamburger joint would be the most obvious choice for nourishment on the go. A standard lunch when travelling would usually consist of a works burger. Ingredients: a beef paddy; cheese; beetroot; tomato; onion; lettuce; BBQ sauce; pineapple, if being indulgent; all nicely layered between a toasted hamburger bun. To wash it down, if a Slurpee wasn't available, my drink of choice was either a chocolate milk or cola soft drink. For dessert, the choice lay with a Chokito or Mars bar. All the sugar, fat, carbs and protein one would need.

Surfing really takes it out of you. It is a real work out, not just physically, with the aerobic and anaerobic exercise, but the sun's rays and saltwater take their toll on the body too. On some days the whole experience is relaxing and calming, yet on other days, due to the waves and conditions, you can cop a beating. But I always experienced a feeling of being cleansed all over. As I have just paused and have loaded up on my lunchtime meal, I might slip into some reflection time. A siesta would be nice too. So, I'll just drift in and out, like the rolling waves and think on some memories of the good old days. The surf safari allows such a carefree existence.

In many Sydney neighbourhoods, at least twice a year, a curb side gutter clean up would be offered by the local council. Back in the seventies and eighties, the local tip was one massive playground of debris. Everything simply left out on the side of the road was destined for landfill. Recycling did later emerge in the eighties, as councils all over feared the rubbish tips would eventually become full. A different type of social consciousness was emerging. On a global scale, serious questioning on what we were doing to the planet was taking hold. In these more modern times, things are very different. Kerbside collection occurs, though everything that can be recycled is done so.

Often "good junk" was thrown out, as piles of household items mounted up in the front of various houses. There were treasures to be had for a lad like me. I loved the week of council clean up. I remember grabbing old pram wheels just around the corner from our place. Sturdy construction, spoked chrome plated steel rims and with white pneumatic tyres with plenty of tread. My imagination was being stoked as I sketched out in my mind the creation of a homemade billy cart. I schemed further and was reminded that, back at home, we always had bits of wood around the house. Nails and screws. And some rope was easy to come by too.

With the aid of my big brother John, and with the hardware we were able to muster, the "green machine" was born from scrap materials. My other older brother Stuart detailed the billy cart, painting it green. A final touch was added by painting a blue lightning bolt down the centre. We were an enterprising family, all quite practical, good with our hands, and possessing creative minds. We were among a generation of thinkers and doers at young ages. My creative hat was never far from my head. And I still keep one eye open these days as I drive through the back streets in my current neighbourhood too. I learnt to make the most of things.

Resilience shone. To turn a negative situation into a positive one was beneficial for me in school, sports, family or friendships. It seemed more favourable than carrying negative feelings around, which would lead to unproductive outcomes. I can confidently state, I was a positive kid. When presented with a nasty situation, I would face it straight on and deal with it confidently. Being a questioning individual was a driving underlying force. Later in life, I have found I still turn negative experiences into positive situations. It has become a bit of an art form, and I use this notion in my counselling and mentoring work.

I accepted Dad's death at a young age, which was extremely hard and painful. Yet, this made other life lessons along the way easier. Sometimes there were reminders of being fatherless, and I missed his presence. Tears would well up in alone times, which was normal, I assured myself. And there were many instances as a young boy, that I wished I had a dad. I was tender on the inside, with a tough exterior, like Astro Boy. This experience set up for me a sense of self-survival. Given a loving family context, and assurances that life would provide.

I have recorded my first ever memory in an essay, while studying my Social Work degree.

"Wow Mitch, a big leap forward! School endeavours must have worked out then!"

"Ha, Ha, yes of sorts," I reply to myself.

As referred to earlier, during my studies, Erickson's Life Cycle Theory explained a great deal to me. I will share the gist of the memory first. I have a visual picture of the event in my mind. I am barely fourteen months old, riding my plastic tot-rod, down our pathway where my dad is burning off some rubbish in the incinerator. This is the house that I was born in, and where my father died at forty-one years. As I was coming down the path, I hopped off my tot-rod and tossed it to the burning flames, where my father was standing. I remember that the toy was yellow.

Whether my memory is accurate is not the point. I may have constructed the memory from fragments of information. It remains a mystery. But within this memory I have pictured my father, and this is significant. My father died when I was only sixteen months old. To be able to hold on to a memory of my father has been important to me through the years. He was real. I have no doubt I will keep this memory for the rest of my life, and it is an anchoring point.

In my dream, I could have been seen as a very naughty boy. I would have been dealt with appropriately for tossing my toy into the fire. And because of this action, denied another tot-rod! My bad, really. A glimmer of the little menace I could be. The activity my dad was doing was burning off garden refuse. I am guessing I was merely interested in the cause and effect. A natural reaction for an impressionable toddler in the company of a dad. Simple modelling and learning.

At home I still have Super Ted, my bear from childhood. The fact that he is still with me sends out a powerful message of the strong bonds of attachment. I even had my nanna design a set of blue denim underpants and cape for him with the letter S. He was a protector figure, and perhaps a projection of myself, and those whose strength protected me during the influential years. He is stripped bare of his superhero costume, power and status now. He simply keeps to himself, perched next to my wife's pink teddy bear, also dearly loved.

It is no surprise, that Ted joined my other superhero, Astro Boy, as a protector figure. Ted was also the name of my pa. Nanna and Pa were grandparents on my mother's side. Nan and Pop were on my dad's side. Having a symbolic visual memory of him, demonstrates the importance of the bonds and attachment I had as a small child. There is a reality for me in that memory of Dad, as well as the monumental sense of loss. But processing these things comes with the territory of being a kid trying to make sense of the world.

On one hand it was easy to say I was liberated by not having a dad growing up. I have lived my life and achieved a great many things without the shadowing of any one dominant male figure. I celebrate that I was able to sample many masculine types from a very young age. For better and for worse, this has helped me become the man and parent I have become.

This is where, while travelling on the surf safari, I need to get out of my head, stop, and survey the beach break. Stopping, breathing and looking out at the horizon is all that is needed. Deciding to just go for it is easy. The East Coast of Australia has the most alluring surfing and swimming spots found anywhere. So, I shall surf for a time and relax.

Now refreshed, I am thinking that a return to the freeway is in order, to gain some ground for a while and pick up speed. I do like to keep moving, and with the window wound down and the wind in my hair, it is wonderful to be travelling in cruise mode again. The Woody is not equipped with much of an air-conditioner. There is something about the rolling wheels too. Momentum for me is calming and liberating. Going somewhere is fun and always brings surprises. So, with some worries behind me, I can put aside some of that deep-seated painful stuff.

Sigmund Freud asserted that the lessons we need to learn will keep coming up before us, until the lesson is learnt. I wonder if we too have a role in what lessons we place before ourselves, and we choose to learn. I would like to think that we would be kind to ourselves and go easy on the whole learning thing by reducing the need for too many harsh lessons, and only tempt ourselves with what we are able to deal with at that life stage. Or to only bite off what we can chew, and swallow. It is our job to savour life experiences. Learning the lessons, experiencing satisfaction, and being courageous in our approach to life are key as we choose or live out our destiny. To be satisfied with lessons placed before ourselves is where peace can be found.

8
Caution the Ripple Which Can Lead to the Riptide

To set the scene, I am hopping out of the Woody and parking it for a while. I recall some earlier modes of transport from my youth and are whizzing through some experiences on bikes: push bikes, 50cc minibikes, moving up to a 125cc motocross bike later. I am now onto my tenth year of adventures, as a young Mitch. The anticipation of my birthday at the beginning of every year is powerful. My enthusiasm was met with the anticipation of a new school year and turning one year older. What newfound challenges would come my way this coming year? The new school year always offered me new realms of opportunity, and stimulation. Regrettably, my world of play, freedom and wonderment was met with a new level of rules.

In 1978, I received a special gift for my birthday from my mother. It was a big kids two-wheeler, a second-hand faded red Malvern Star push bike. A beauty. These were before BMX bikes were invented. I even remember the family who we acquired it from. I had entered the world of the big boys, an important milestone for an impressionable lad in those days. As a child it is always on to the next thing. Maybe that was my take on life. I was not a child who was forever wanting things. Rather, I was fit for what life was ready to throw at me, full of passion, energy and life.

I was grounded, though, in gratitude for what I did have in my possession. My Christian education gave me purpose, humility and a set of guiding values. I was not a greedy kid. I do remember praying to God, asking to receive a minibike, seeing I had mastered the push bike. I was not bored with the Malvern Star bike, I just needed to master the next machine in line. I was perhaps fuelled by some real get up and go, all the time.

This time though, with my prayer life so active too, I was going to put in a sizable order and move to the next level up. I had been taught to pray to God: "Ask and you shall receive." I knew Santa was a close runner up in putting forward my request, and he had delivered on previous occasions. I was prepared to give it all to make a wish like this come true. I have strong memories of making this wish known, and considerable effort on my part was made to publicise my wishes. Having developed a good prayer life over the years, I told myself to have faith that such a request would be granted.

Like many positive experiences in my childhood, my

mother was the primary instigator, like that of the Malvern Star bike. She may not have been fully aware of the deep significance of this dream. I can recall one adventure of riding a two-wheeler minibike during my early years, at a church fellowship picnic. Mum arranged the whole family outing. I am sure she had a good idea that my wish list included a minibike. I had provided so much detail, battering her ear drums most of the time.

This experience was after many enthusiastic prayer sessions to almighty God and extended wish-making efforts to Santa as well. A couple of years had lapsed. Obtaining a motorised mini trail bike did come. It was not from Santa's bag of toys. A pillow slip could not hide a minibike in the lounge room. As a child, I believed God and Santa must have been in cahoots with each other. And perhaps Mum played a part.

This particular year, around twelve years of age, we were gathered for a church fellowship picnic day, in Glenworth Valley near Wisemans Ferry. My family and I, along with many of the hip fellowship group, were having fun. It was at this event that I had my first minibike experience. We drove down a mountain ridge into the valley, where there was an oval-shaped track, carved out of the landscape. It had been worn away from the minibikes ripping around. They immediately caught my attention as they sped single file in an anti-clockwise direction. The other activities such as horse riding, swimming and the picnic itself were dwarfed by the glorious minibikes hooning around.

I remember Andrew and I were so thrilled to get a go on these little beauties. My other brothers were too big for these bikes and went off riding horses. This was an activity that was so significant for me and has become one of those stand out childhood memories. It is always a big deal when you do something for the first time. From the experience at Wisemans Ferry, and a few more minibike riding turns at various other places, I grew drawn more and more to the activity. The motorised bike thing grew into a passion for me. The time came when I obtained my very own trail bike, which I purchased with my own money: the Suzuki RM 125 two stroke. Team colours of blue and yellow, of course. This was in the early eighties, and I was loving it!

My love for motorbikes was real and happening before my very own eyes. At this point of my early teen development, I embarked upon a whole new set of skills, thrills and spills. I found an element of freedom, which accompanied me and my mates as we journeyed into the world of adolescence. The couple of years I spent enjoying the trail bike with all my misadventures were the greatest. They were years packed with so much adventure. There was never a moment to spare. It was jam-packed.

My turbulent teens were drawing closer, though I was oblivious. Living in the moment was my reality, not how my next day or week would play out. I was heading for something quite unexpected, which would hit me front on and with full force. When riding a bike, I kept it steady, hanging on with a firm grip, and negotiated the terrain before me. I never knew what was around the bend. The thrill, excitement and anticipation of what was coming next allowed me to ride on the edge of my seat. I have always carried determination in my backpack. From mowing the lawns, and my weekly chores, I had earnt the money to buy the Suzuki RM 125. I was proud of my second-hand possession. It was clapped out but worked, made a hell of a sound, and transported me where I needed to go.

My childhood was enmeshed in a loving family, many family friends, and a community where my developing years supported the notion of safety and wellbeing. There was an element of risk taking, but the platform provided by the commitment of my mother, immediate and extended family provided a sure foundation where I was able to continue the process of laying the blocks, layering and firming up my identity. Childhood was wonderful and packed full. I was never left wanting or feeling I was missing out. Growing up in a one parent, matriarchal run household had an element of uniqueness to it. I loved my family.

My primary years led to the exploration of my adolescent beginnings, loaded with experiences and misadventures.

Who really knows why certain events occur and unfold, and for what reasons we are given the opportunities to discover later the lessons? The choices I took had consequences and led to the different paths I chose. It is necessary for me to understand how I framed the circumstances in which I found myself. The very solid foundations that were laid for me by others, and by myself also, provided a firm foundation from which to construct and begin building a sense of myself. This was crucial to my later survival, to not falling into a victim state of being.

In later life, when there were many curve balls thrown at me, there was often resilience in the fabric of me that was being formed. The weave and weft, alike to the metaphor of construction. A gentler notion is that the binding each of us undertakes is a strengthening process, indeed enables us for our future encounters. The exploration and unpacking of events in my childhood reveals much in my own ability to deal with life. A positive childhood across the years tethered me carefully, despite the early loss of Dad, and Mum's failed second marriage. It tested the fabric and shook the foundations.

There will be tears, rips and cracks that appear, but we call forth the handy person from within ourselves. And perhaps also, bring on the developing inner hero waiting to emerge and see us on our way again. From me, the little boy became a young person. At this stage of life,

I was preparing for the next learning experience and adventure. It wasn't until many years after that I realised the importance and value attributed to the days and years growing up participating in the many activities that I have described so far. The self-appointed little boy-come-superhero was emerging as a best friend, while sitting on his own shoulder surveying the world around. There was a feeling of contentment, coupled with the wonderment of "what next?" Anticipation!

9
Moral Compass and Misdemeanours

As one of four boys, you might imagine we all had our fair share of rubbing up against each other. That passive image belies the vigorous nature of our interactions. Growing up, we shared some character similarities, and also some very different individual strengths. There would be times where we would complement each other, and other moments where the testosterone levels would erupt, causing trouble in all directions. My mother could have told many stories involving our behaviour, and my brothers would each remember other scraps of memory from those days together.

I have a clear memory of one typical fight between my two elder brothers. My younger brother and I were mere observers on this occasion. A disagreement had erupted, and the chase commenced. Faster they ran from one end of the house to the other. The final blow was thrown just as the bedroom door was slammed shut. What followed was a clenched, full-fisted blow-smack into the middle section of the hollow core door. The crack and denting of the plywood were proof of such brotherly love and strength. The brother whose room it was ended up slapping a large Superman sticker over the top.

My mother had a job ahead of her, and she often reminded us of this: "Jan and her four boys." I did get it, the job thing. It was performed with enormous love and devotion. Those who knew her would not deny her legendary status. Raising a family does reflect a work ethic and, in my own family, I have drawn much on my mother's work ethic. As a parent of two boys, I appreciate the role and effort needed to rear children. My wife and partner-in-crime are committed to the process of parenting, as we journey as a family unit together. We are lucky, as we have not suffered losses like my mother, and are both providers.

My emerging faith at this part of the journey was very tangible. I shall begin to weave this part of me into my story. As I reflect on the values and morals imparted to me by my mother, family and friends, it became clear that life was bridled with an understanding that there was more to this living thing than any of my family and friends could sum up. Through an understanding of faith, I knew there was more to life than I could put my finger on. Being "a good boy" and "doing the right thing" were an important starting point of the equation.

Values and morals were being shaped around God. Additionally, fostering a deep-seated spirituality which originated in a Christian context led to a strong sense of social justice, and love for my neighbour. I was learning to consider others, while finding my place in the world. I felt that good things would come my way, if I kept my end of the bargain. This was the introduction to something outside of myself.

Learning to pray, in my infant years, was not dissimilar to making a wish list for Santa. It was much better to participate in this than to question too hard. The hereditary Christian faith formed a firm backdrop. My grandparents and mother attended church services, both in the Methodist and Presbyterian denominations. The Uniting Church emerged from both. I have fond memories growing up, active in the local congregations. My childhood enabled me to share in many people's lives. The church communities were integral.

Participation gave me a firm platform from which to explore other Christian experiences, such as Anglican Youth. I attended school holiday camps where my faith was able to deepen, due to the rich and wonderful experiences, from the age of eight. The times away in parts of New South Wales and Queensland introduced me to friendships with a wide range of people. We would communicate by letter and phone during the school term to arrange which camps we would all enrol in for the holiday period.

Many adults volunteered their time, demonstrating

practical ministry of the Christian faith. It was a wonderful period of my life. My association lasted ten years, and in later years I became a volunteer myself, then an employee as a professional instructor in outdoor education, providing camping experiences for schools and holiday groups.

The camping experiences through my childhood and teens came about in the wake of my older brothers attending the camps. I listened to their stories as they swapped them with each other. Back at home, Mum commenced the arduous task of loading the washing machine. She was a great concurrent listener, and would hear their stories, comment, and ask questions, while completing the job of the laundry efficiently.

My brother's stories inspired me, and I too wanted to participate in the adventures they experienced while on camp. I now appreciate that having a break from fulltime caring would have been great respite for my mother too. Having us all go off for a week provided her with a break from our hectic family life. Mum knew we had positive experiences. Her limited budget would stretch to the demands of the camp each was most attracted to. She respected our individual differences and tried to accommodate our wishes without loading us up with her money struggles.

I remember fondly the forms that we would look at, deciding which set of camping experiences we would like to do. I never worried about going off to the camps as they were good, safe fun. From the morning gathering at Central Station, curiosity and wonderment surrounded every kid. It now reminds me of the time when Harry Potter meets all the other students on the train station preparing to venture into their experience with other classmates entering Hogwarts School of Witchcraft and Wizardry.

One special Camp Howard camping experience is etched in my mind. Travelling by train, I was destined for the campsite located at Gerroa's Seven Mile Beach. There, I met a special girl and, over the following days, sustained a severe crush. This relationship was rekindled each camping experience, with much coordination prior to the school holiday with phone calls ensuring there would be a common camping destination locked in for the both of us. Gerroa, and the many fond memories, will always have a special place in my heart. And it was a great region for surfing too.

After each camping adventure at Gerroa and other sites—relationship catch-ups, fond encounters, and break-ups along the way—our close group of regular campers would return home with a euphoria resulting from the experiences shared. The subsequent low and let down upon re-entering the normal conditions of everyday life brought about a disheartened commencement of my beckoning school term. A world away from the humdrum of normal routine, the memories of those seven days each year seemed eternal.

Encounters that supported positive learning capturing many of life's lessons were pitched within the context of a temporary community setting. The facilities boasted common halls, shared cabins or tents, communal eating of notoriously splendid camp food, daily devotions and worship. These were packed either side of great outdoor activities such as archery, canoeing, hiking, farm visits, surfing, and sailing. Gerroa was marked by craft teaching and genuine care. Well-resourced by a few very special individuals, the craft room was my own place of respite while away.

On another campsite I learnt to sail. Sailing was another pursuit that I took to with passion, and it was ignited through my early camping experiences on the beautiful Port Hacking River in the Royal National Park, south of Sydney. Positive mentoring on the waterways gave me experience in all types of weather conditions. I became confident on different types of sailing dinghies, fiberglass and timber sixteen-foot skiffs, Flying Elevens, and Corsairs. The skilled leaders provided a positive environment, and I became competent in boat handling, crewing and skippering. An appreciation of the maintenance and care of various watercraft came later.

10
Deeper and Down

A new life stage was upon me. I invited God into my life. I embarked upon a literal crusade at this point in my young years. This choice nestled in a greater understanding of myself, and the bigger picture of life. Doors were opening to the world around me. My conversion in the Christian faith was one still of mystery but also grounded, and an action that made sense. As a twelve-year-old, my understanding of a personal faith was grasped eagerly. Over the next few years, this evolved into a deeper relationship with my God, one that would add an important dimension in my life.

I am still full of questions, but a real relationship with God is a crucial part of who I am. Going back to the time of my conversion, I can recall a sort of naivety, which highlighted my innocence in a sense. Conversely, I experienced a knowing of great magnitude around this concept of conversion within the Christian faith. It was faith with purpose and real belief. It was another initiation, and a new beginning of personal development. I embraced the defining journey of conscious choice making, packed with questions and a search for meaning.

I believe books come to you at the right moment. I was introduced to the book *A Fresh Start*, which provided crucial inspiration. Reading had never really featured for me, except in hearing bedtime stories as a much younger child. My mother would also read some great stories, including biblical ones. After late primary school, my theoretical thinking, coupled with growing confidence, developed.

At twelve, we all participated in reading aloud with some trepidation. My fear of reading came from being in Sunday school classes, where we would share quotes and read bible stories. I was very self-conscious of my reading inability and would often hide behind the fact that I was not a confident reader. My awkwardness allowed me to be myself. I was warmly accepted and did move on over time to have confidence in reading. The fact that it was a small, intimate group of young people meant that we were learning acceptance of each other in our local congregation.

The feeling once I had read *A Fresh Start* for myself was enormous. I felt proud that I could give a book review later at a Christian camp. I was confident in standing up in front of the group of kids and leaders, and to be able to give my account of its worth. There was a sense of power in doing that review. This book also carried deep insights for living well, ones I wanted to share with others. I was proud to be a young Christian.

Great lessons in sailing took me deeper again. My great enjoyment of sailing was partially due to allowing the wind as a force of nature to propel me, slipping through the seas. Feeling the spray from the caps of the ocean wash over me was a reminder of how wonderful the great outdoors really is. Under the guidance of supportive and skilled adult sailors, I blossomed. Once the days of being an apprentice at learning to sail were rounded off, I was able to develop the skills, ability and motivation to make it in most weather conditions.

A dream, though, was to go it alone one day and test my seafaring skills in a single-handed boat. I bought an older timber nine-foot scow from a school friend. I had again worked and saved enough to purchase this rather tired old thing. I spent many weeks sanding it back, and re-painting the hull and deck in bright colours. It looked snazzy by the time it was ready to sail. Sailing my little moth, "Good One," as I named it, would cap off this period and chapter of youth, filled with all sorts of learning, adventures, racing, and misadventures. I am "skippering" ahead here though.

A timber cradle was constructed for Good One by my carpenter brother, which hoisted it into the roof of our garage, and lowered the boat onto the car for transport. My mother was the one to drive the much-loved contraption.

Having been introduced to the sport of sailing in my early camping years, I took to it in a big way in my late primary school years and into early high school years. Prior to me obtaining Good One, I experienced a unique relationship with another budding sailor friend. In Year Seven, together with my crew mate Adam and his dad, I purchased our first sailing dingy: a Flying Eleven, called "Mach-1." It was second-hand and in reasonable condition. It just needed a good scrub down, the purchase of a new main and jib sheet. The Flying Eleven class allowed two budding new sailors to learn all aspects of the sport.

It had a main sail, jib and spinnaker. We were able to learn the art of setting and trimming the sails and rigging in all weather conditions to bring about optimal performance for the craft. The hull was fiberglass, a sleek and flowing design. However, the Flying Eleven still tended to feel like a bathtub once capsized. Water would fill the dinghy, and then not easily drain out. But we soon learned to deal with capsizing, bailing water, keeping the nose of the boat into the wind, and watching for the luffing sails and boom.

The Flying Eleven is a racing class, and the season unfolded through spring and summer, weekly each Sunday. The water of Pittwater, north of Sydney, would get very busy at times with so many boats and watercraft enjoying the beautiful warm days. We gained the skills for conducting ourselves safely and had enormous fun. We were given instruction regularly, but mostly our skills were picked up from simply being out on the water and coping with whatever presented.

On one occasion our mainstay snapped, and the mast toppled down. Panic ensued, until we were able to paddle and drift onto a remote part of the foreshore for safety. The episode left us unable to recommence the race. We were what seemed the tailenders of the fleet in our sailing skills and experience in the early days. However, we had many good laughs and attempts at racing which did give us more confidence and abilities along the way, standing us in good stead. We also learned not to take ourselves too seriously.

I remember one day when another team of older kids, more experienced in rigging and sailing, assisted us in fine-tuning our boat prior to the race. We found ourselves in a favourable position on this leg of the course, after working hard and tacking with precision to keep up with the fleet. Before we knew it, we were neck and neck with the guys that assisted us in the rigging and setting up of our boat earlier. They were known champions. We took them with great excitement at the turn of the next buoy, but it was short lived. They eventually took us again on a downwind leg later in the race, but it felt good to have defeated them on one leg of the course.

In hindsight, the days of sailing provided many metaphors on how we live life. It was not an activity for the faint-hearted, and required commitment, survival and the development of specific skills. In order to develop real confidence, I had to not only navigate and skipper a vessel relying on the wind for the only source of power but be prepared to take on anything that may have arisen along the journey. There were times when quick action working as a team allowed us to overcome and pull through.

When it comes to sailing, all the equipment, right down to the last shackle, needs to be working, and life can depend on it. Most importantly, this life metaphor of my sailing days, when having to weather a storm, or when afloat at sea, shows that confidence is needed in your vessel and the skipper. The mind frame that I can get myself safely back to shore is central. Sailing is about endurance. I must be my own skipper to sail the intended course. One must trust in oneself and finding inner strength is crucial.

Having a securely attached lifeline in the case of extreme mishaps as I explored my world was a needed thing. This enabled me to feel safe enough for just enough freedom to begin with, and the right amount of risk too. I thought I was doing it all for myself. But there seemed to be someone who was on watch for this kid. I remember there was much faith invested into me. Love in action and watchfulness seemed to go hand in hand

Love often travels with us lifelong if done correctly. The life raft or rescue boat was never far away in my case, and by allowing discovery of myself, I was never hampered by my family and friends. Giving way to a fun-filled period of self-discovery, in environments where even mistakes were all part of the journey, was blessed. It was a buoyant, positive period, adding significantly to the bank of positive memories. The active learning I encountered in the early stages of my youth have taught me how necessary the stacking of positive memories is. Positive memories create solid anchorage and can hold a vessel firm.

"Stormy weather" is an important part of the mix of conditions we must accept and face as part of growing up. As kids, strands of resilience can be positively woven into the fabric which helps us face those testing winds and conditions in the future. The cloth of life is never going to be unbreakable. Life equals vulnerability, but where resilience can be taught, and learned, it strengthens us for future times. Hopefully we all learn the power of participation. Change and choice go hand in hand when using the tiller. Navigation is not always easy. But a destination is very helpful.

11
A Bit of a Mess

I now need to set the scene at the age of fifteen turning sixteen. This is as a way of really warming up to providing my own confession later of what was foolish behaviour. My actions leading to guilt have plagued me for a long time. I accept that the role in making certain choices was mine. An experience at the young-but-not-so-young age of fifteen years had consequences. I was no longer a child at this point of my decision making. Innocence featured far less, but my natural rebellion was taking root.

Knowingly, I experimented with what seemed to be harmless and socially acceptable in some circles: marijuana, pot, grass, or weed. Given the stage of life I was experiencing, marijuana was the typical first choice of serious experimental drug taking. Except for cigarettes, and alcohol. I might add that a high percentage of young people, and my peers, were experimenting with these drugs in varying degrees.

Studies in recent years have shown the damage and

mental health issues associated with smoking pot, especially for those who are susceptible. Now it is the case for these individuals that there can be harmful, long-lasting ill effects for life. In my current work, I hear people explain how they regret using drugs, and are living with mental anguish as a result of their choices. I have seen the damage drugs cause to individuals and families in all social demographic circles. I now see how both hard and recreational drug use has had detrimental ramifications on physical and mental health. Addiction has even caused death.

I was a well-known and popular kid in my community, and my experimental actions sent a strong message to other kids and parents. The ill effects of the choices I made were shockingly known through my community. My dabbling resulted in a full-on disruption to the early beginnings of a charted life. It further sent a ripple effect throughout the school community. These substances did in fact have a great effect on my health, despite only using pot on a few occasions. I was sharply made aware of my vulnerability very quickly. My life had taken one of those unexpected turns, as I knowingly made the choice to experiment, and ended up a casualty.

In an artwork much later in life, I expressed the view that any experience can be thought of as either a nightmare, or a dream, or both. The consequences of one's choices and actions do bear outcomes that can lead to regret down the track. By smoking illegal substances, I suffered a nervous breakdown, ending up confused in, and disoriented with, the world. After forty-eight hours of internal chaos, I found myself involuntarily committed as a patient in a mental health unit. Traumatic does not even begin to explain how I was feeling. I was left to work out for myself, and for those around me, what the hell happened.

My family witnessed all that came as a result of this fall, and how this disabling juvenile experience made life difficult. Their actions, love and support did not fail. In one way I was just like any other fifteen-year-old grappling with adolescence and the turbulence it brings. However, surviving a mental breakdown did bring a deeper dimension to it all, an unexplainable dimension to my life. Even in a supported family environment, with the backing of a neighbourhood of families and a strong supportive community that I loved, my life became so complicated and challenging. It was no easy task to live through this psychosis. Central to the journey has been sharing my mistakes, and forgiving myself.

I eventually received a diagnosis of affective bipolar disorder at the age of sixteen. I was now under care of a psychiatrist, and the support of the state hospital system. But I have gone on regardless, living my life, stoking dreams, setting goals and working hard to bring about new directions. I have learnt never to give up, and at those times when it's too hard, I have gained the insight to give it over to someone I trust for support. Accepting help is a courageous thing to do.

The road ahead was uncertain for some time. I could not see anything but fog for many months. As my recovery moved through the different phases, I knew I had to keep going and move on. The fact that I was never one to remain idle for long stood me in good stead, as did the inner drive in me. I needed to be mobile once again. But the irony is, I was not yet set to move on. My life post-psychosis was the beginning of a new life of sorts. I needed to have a lot of time-out, and struggled with deep mood swings of depression over many years. There were deep thinking times throughout the depressive moods.

One of most important messages I can offer is the act of reaching out. If you are someone who can recognise depression in others, then reach out to them. If you are someone suffering depression, accept the help by breaking the conspiracy of silence. The offer of one hand or voice seeking to contact with another can make all the difference. Many years on, the struggle to just get on with it, and live to the best of my ability, has been about setting goals, and breaking down the tasks within them. Setting goals is paramount, even if it is in my head only. Having an achievable destination in sight and mind helps, as does finding your rhythm.

To use analogies from several movies. In *The Wizard of Oz*, the young character Dorothy reminds us that it all starts with a single step. Even if that step leads to a stumble. The most famous of sayings is: "Just pick yourself up, dust yourself off—and start all over again" Oh, different movie. That one is from *Calamity Jane*. The real journey begins with putting things behind oneself. When a newborn baby takes its first steps of life, the little creature starts from a crawl to a bum slide, to knees, to wobbly feet. They may just need propping up at times, during those first groping steps.

Within the various fields of science, there are now many discoveries into understanding brain function, and developments are occurring so rapidly in the twenty-first century. There are advancements in pharmacological treatments and natural therapies, the functional approaches of proven psychological interventions, and greater public interest in mental health issues. These in turn have attracted greater political recognition and funding opportunities, resulting in better overall support for individuals and families alike. Good mental health is crucial to having an equitable, functioning society.

I have been able to build on further research in study I have undertaken. Working in the field of mental health as a career choice, my ambition is to couple such interest with the insights I have gained from living with a mental illness. I would like to think I can contribute to the bigger picture of understanding mental health. But I also know that just being me, myself and I is significant enough within the communities I am already active in. Maybe this book could be a beginning, not just for my own wellbeing, but for others living with the challenges of mental illness.

All that aside, I graduated from university with a Bachelor of Social Work. Within that course, I took units of psychology and sociology. At university, we were shown a series of short documentary-style sociological and psychological experiments that tried to prove the ability of three-year-old children to lie. The experiment highlighted a set of circumstances where children had already learned to lie. From a young age, we can determine real outcomes through the choices we make, and the formulation of self appears coupled with choice.

As a developing juvenile, I was in a process of looking forward and back, as well as to the side. I embarked upon misadventures in my early teen years. The road ahead meant a crossing over from young juvenile ways to young adult ways. Bicycle motocross, BMX, was the emerging, in-thing for boys in those days. This sport brought with it many skills, thrills, and spills—and enabled a freedom of expression for many of my mates and myself. But, as the period just prior to getting a learner driver's license loomed, the push bike riding was soon to be replaced with the thrill of being able to drive a car. A new responsibility was ushering me into the future. Before the onset of too much responsibility, I peddled my way with some radical manoeuvring on my diamond frame BMX.

I have always been a very visual person. I love movies, especially *Good Will Hunting*. Robin Williams was very skilled in playing the role of a mildly disillusioned therapist. He is depicted as living a comfortable life and has a teaching role in the field of psychology at the local community college. The extremely bright client Will, played by Matt Damon, begins therapy, and it proves quite challenging for the therapist in the early stages of their relationship. The story unfolds as the two people form a meaningful therapeutic bond through the context of the mandatory therapy sessions.

I identified parallels in the movie to my own life, as I have had invaluable medical support and powerful psychological mentoring along my own journey of recovery. When Will is sprouting how much knowledge he had gained from reading philosophical, psychological and sociological literature, he sought to emphasise his intelligence to the therapist. The warm psychologist, whose own journey is also played out, humours Will by recognising that Will's experiences in life are limited, bringing awareness to Will that he has primarily theoretical experience of life to date. The therapist, in conversation with Will, leads him to discover more about himself. We see the powerful and delicate realisation of a recovery journey of a very bright young individual through the help of a kindred spirit.

My psychosis, or "break down," as it was referred to then, had me reframe this period of my life in a big way. Only in later life have I been able to track back into childhood to prod and pry into my behaviours. Contributing to the stressors around the time of being fifteen and sixteen, I believe the psychosis was triggered by the smoking of pot. Being informed that I might have a predisposition to bipolar has also provided some explanation.

12
Digging Myself Out of the Hole

This account of my journey may be of interest if you are indeed a young person: younger, or simply young of heart. In this book, I have tried to relate to people, whatever their background, persuasion, and position in life. I also acknowledge that all of us have experienced turbulence in our lives. I am hoping that reading this touches a few chords and encourages you to share your own memories. I admit that I have been happy to shake some of those rattling bones of the skeletons in the closet. It may be good for you to address some things too?

At the time of the psychosis, I was experiencing mental exhaustion, and system shut down was imminent. Time out was forced upon me at this crucial juvenile stage of life. To this day, I emphasise the confusion of all that embraces a kid growing into a young, then adult, person. It is a strange and mysterious period of life, full of unexpected adventures and pathways. It was an enormous and disturbing spin out for me though. I was tired now at sixteen, and in a way my depression has been a friend ever since. I have never written that before in describing this condition.

The rhythm and rhyme that writing has provided for me, having journalled for over twenty-five years about my life with a bipolar condition, , has enabled me to beat my own drum, privately. A life at an early age dealing with mood swings of depression and elation began as challenging. For most young people the "growing up" experience entails a normal pattern of ebb and flow of moods and emotions and is subject to turmoil periodically.

My road trip in the Kingswood, has taken me to some great surf locations at this point. I have had some great moments in the sun and sea, and salt air. The ocean is still life-giving and a healthy place to spend time. The return trip to home and a conventional lifestyle is now on my mind too. The endless summer is but a pipe dream. I know fear, and I know how to move through it now. I had to learn this, to think fearlessly, and to feel emotional pain on occasions. It has taken time. Work, and effort. I built a work ethic around addressing my mental health.

As a juvenile, fear of varying degrees existed in many corners of life. There were stand-out firsts in merging into the adult world. Growing through this young adult period led to feeling disoriented and forced a deep questioning of how I defined myself. Living with a mental illness, I was walking unfamiliar ground. Turning the mirror towards myself was very scary. I had done some mirroring in my junior years, when considering my leap of faith into Christianity. This time, I saw a fractured reflection, a shattered image, and a task of not knowing how to mend.

I was forced to depart high school in Term One of Year Ten. My absence from school was due to being admitted into hospital. I was now a young patient living in the psychiatric ward of the district hospital and spent my birthday in a zombie-like state. Upon admission, I was treated for my recent psychosis, and later found out that the medical team was unsure about the best treatment pathway for me. I presented as a mystery, and there were many unknowns to the puzzle. I had no previous history of mental illness, and many medical interventions were applied during the following weeks. For now, time was on my side.

Whether I wanted to be there or not, I was having to ride this out. I cannot remember having the capacity to question anything at this acute stage. I was under sedation from strong anti-psychotic medications. I was safe, numb, and just existing. The following weeks on the ward served to offer some insight for the medical team, but the complete picture was not clear from this first-time admission. After many weeks in rehabilitation, being exposed to various combinations of medication, and even electro-convulsive treatment, my state of mind returned to some degree of normalcy.

Finally, the stabilisation of my mood meant I was able to return home. I was under instruction to take some green tablets, a white and a red one, each day and night. I was still sedated, and bewildered. I remember waiting for my mother to take me away from this place, and I departed knowing I was a changed person.

Upon my discharge, there was a compassionate community health team and daily support provided. I engaged in this program for as long as I needed it during the following months. It was a positive experience with committed, friendly staff helping my recovery. The staff supported me, and many other people attending the program, through several activities, social meetings, and outings. The months of that first post-psychosis year were overwhelmingly hectic and numbing. It was a dream-like state. At this point, having my car to drive was ultimately the best thing for me, and crucial to my sanity.

Still dazed with the events of the first nine months of that year, I was soon ready to begin the emotional return journey back to my familiar self. My family were shell-shocked that year. They would have been equally taken back and looking for directions at this stage too. I received family support from a close aunt and uncle. I was able to spend time yet again on another campsite operated by the Uniting Church. I slowly oriented myself back to health through light duties with my uncle on the campsite, building on my work ethic for my own better mental health. The peaceful surrounds of the bush and staff helped in my recovery journey that year. But there was something always propelling me in a forward direction. I am not sure if this was faith, my own strength, my determination or the courage of my convictions? Something. There was something in the fabric that kept my sail set. The weave and weft of the fabric hung together. I was finally able to catch a gust and charter a fresh course. I was not giving up!

Recovery is an ongoing process. The harsh reality that there is no cure for affective bipolar 1 mental illness had not impacted on me yet. I was constantly and urgently in a wakening state of mind, questioning where to from here as I worked out how to grapple with my new health condition.

Maybe this was my saving grace: I was always seeking the next thing. This kept me moving, rather than being bogged down in sorrow. Having a sense of traction through mobilisation of myself was a blessing. Between sixteen and seventeen, I had the task of creating my own mental rebuild. I reflected that I probably had the "right stuff" to do it. I embraced the solid platform of childhood resilience. I just needed some direction.

Back to the story, and the theme of transporting myself. My first car was a blessing beyond belief. I was behind the wheel of not only a great classic first-time vehicle, but it enabled me to make safe trips of my own making. Under a provisional license, I had as much freedom as I needed, and I began to set about making my own small trips. Independence through driving was one of life's biggest privileges and milestones. The vehicle that I became so proud of was a faded blue Volkswagen six-volt manual sedan Type 3. Not a Beetle, but a sedan Type 3. Quite a rare piece of motoring history!

My great mate, Bruce, at the time was in possession of this little beauty. It was one car among an array of other projects at his house. One day, I was present when a conversation broke out between Bruce and his mum. She was fed up with the cars parked in her driveway. Not wasting an opportunity I spoke up, stating I would buy the Type 3 Volkswagen. "Done!" shouted Barbara. However, there was one condition. Bruce was not one to let go so easily, explained that it needed mechanical work, and that it was unregistered. He proposed that no money be exchanged and, following my work in getting the car back on the road, he would just borrow the car now and then when he needed it. I scoffed at the thought. Tight-lipped, and with a horrified look, he accepted the cash. The compassion of this family was unmatched during my recovery. We enjoyed years of friendship.

Things were looking brighter. This period was coupled with joy and great challenge, making small headway.

The following months, I managed to balance everything: study, work, car expenses, and more responsibilities. There were new kinds of adult stressors. I felt as if I was trying to scramble up a shifting mountain face, climbing with barely anything, desperately trying to stop myself from falling. As I grasped onto any solid formation with sheer determination and strength, I did not fully realise I had more tools, life skills and support under my belt to take on such a challenge.

The diagnosis of having bipolar disorder came as a relief. Not knowing what your mind state is, and the mechanics of its functioning, is hard going. Although it had a name, it was completely unknown territory. My diagnosis had come unexpectedly from my visits to a private psychiatrist. Following a few short consultations, including attempting a psychometrics test, I was provided with the answer. Lithium was to be at the core of the treatment plan from a pharmacological perspective. The heavy anti-psychotics and tranquilisers were replaced with this white powdered tablet, which is still considered as one of the gold standard treatments for bipolar today. My health did now start to improve.

The Power of One, by Bryce Courtney is a great example of a story where strength is depicted beautifully. It resonated with me on many levels. Also, in mental health recovery, it is vital to be strong. I coined the phrase for myself,

"Tomorrow is another day," and some days I needed enough strength to believe things would get better. I would tell myself, and write in my diary, that whatever is going on for me presently is simply just that. I learnt that moods do move on. Eventually tomorrow comes and brings hope of something else. In between, sleep was a godsend.

To give you a picture of a deep depression, I could be in bed for anything up to as long as twelve weeks. This would follow a period of escalating elation and mania usually. The mania mood state was much shorter, as I mostly grew able to sense when my mood was escalating. Insight into my moods developed. Following the use of heavy tranquilisers, my body would simply slow. It was like a switch would be thrown, and then: lights out. I would collapse into the mood of depression. This was repair time for body, mind, spirit. During those dark times, I had no choice but to repair. Little energy was present, and few things could move me from my bed. It was like sleeping under a lead blanket.

The support of my mother, dutifully administering my medication morning and night, would finally bring me about and lift my mood. The introduction of strong antidepressants always featured during these times. The art of knowing when to introduce what medication and the strength required was initiated by my doctor. Over time, I learnt how to recognise the signs as well, and remained active in my medication management. Developing good insight into how the moods played out, and understanding the power of the different medications, is what made managing things easier.

Much later in life I have learnt a thing called mindfulness. A different, powerful and important lesson to live in the moment. In lighter moods, applying mindfulness is certainly a worthy tool for the recovery journey.

Developing a mind strength, even in the early times, was crucial. Even though it took years to properly manage things, my mind strength grew from a variety of sources, and would eventually become an artform. Practicing the creativity of art was a profound way to bring a mindfulness state. As I practiced more art over the years, even making surfboards, I slowly learnt to live creatively across other life domains.

Imagination is magical, and the beginning of good things comes from positive thinking, actions, and belief. My world was expanding, and I began believing in myself. This new world I was now thrust into was opening doors, and conversations with people often served as signposts. Relationships can open doorways and lead us to exciting places and unknown territories. The mere action of taking such bold steps often rewarded me greatly. Learning to live creatively was satisfying, as I took hold of fostering a healthy and strong mind.

During my sixteenth, seventeenth, and eighteenth years, new challenges were to confront me. I had tried to re-enrol at school in the remaining few months of Year Ten. This proved difficult, as I had missed so much schoolwork. I chose to formally leave and seek some other training and work outside of school. My mother placed a condition upon me, which was at the bare minimum to obtain my School Certificate. I enrolled in TAFE for the final semester of 1984 to commence this equivalent qualification.

As I was now driving, I needed money for fuel, as well as pocket money. I spent some time repairing surfboards for the local shaper and surf shop owner, then commenced working in the local service station as a driveway service assistant on a casual basis. I loved the job and, in my other spare time, would provide general labour for my brother's building business. My brilliant stroke of luck in the very late stage of 1984 was achieving a three-month trial over Christmas and into the new year with a local boat builder. He was prepared to indenture me as an apprentice at the end of this period, should our working relationship work out for "both of us."

As I faded from my service station role, I began full-time work in the small-time boat building factory located in the Northern Beaches suburb of Narrabeen. I began the year with all bases loaded. The new year saw me studying my certificate course three nights a week. I was working as a boat builder, and I would soon commence one day a week at TAFE in Ultimo for the trade course also. Without the possession and use of my car, I could not have achieved such optimistic results. After months of trying, and working hard in the boat building job, I was offered the apprenticeship.

However, I turned it down. I was recognised for my hand skills, keen eye, knowledge and perception on the job. However, I felt that I needed a bigger company context to develop my trade seriously. The current establishment was a husband-and-wife team, and I needed a broader experience base. I now saw myself as someone of worth. I had skills, and I was contributing. I was forging something of a new identity for myself.

13
The Wordsmith at Work, the Decision to Write

I am sure you have heard someone use the saying they will have to "hit the ground running." To me the saying implies that the time to start has already passed, and that the individual is required to be operating at maximum speed. There is no lead time. I see an image of the cartoon character the Roadrunner. We never saw his legs when he was running because they were always drawn in full spinning motion. He was followed by a swirl of dust that followed.

There was dust at my heels as I manoeuvred through the year. It seemed that I too had hit the ground fast when it came to engaging in all my activities. There was a sense of making up for lost time. True to form I was ambitious, yes, but cautious, no. The question remained whether I had imposed upon myself an unrealistic schedule. Whatever the answer at this stage, although it was hard work, I was loving the feeling of moving forward with speed. To be in full throttle in life again felt great.

I was experiencing numerous new insights into my revamped life and had no time to spare. I was a free agent, with a car, an apprenticeship, my adult education studies, trade course, and the typical social life of a young seventeen-year-old. I had not a care in the world and was experiencing a moment of temporary release. I had no reason to fear, nor doubt good things were ahead.

With my school buddies on one side, and fellowship and church friends on the other, I enjoyed life like any other young person, who was burgeoning into adulthood. I was beginning to know a new me. Despite this euphoria, I carried a fragility in my being. I had it like an acute awareness. While I saw a new dimension of myself, there was a vulnerability. The robust Mitch pre-breakdown had been replaced with an unsettling sense of exposure to forces outside me. But to compensate, I now carried a maturity that was missing before. I had a different type of respect for myself. However, with little to no experience living well with a mental illness, I was not wise enough to see the writing on the wall.

With many new experiences, and at the pace that I was living my life, came many new stressors. I did not recognise these experiences as potentially harmful. However, these stressors invariably proved too much during these months of my newfound potential and endless options. The new medications provided some stability, though did not provide an iron clad insurance of not having future mood swings. I was not aware that this was the case at the time, and I was blinded to the reality I was to face.

I was in constant contact with my psychiatrist, trying to hone the dosages of the medications that now governed my physiology. Learning about the different side effects, changes to my body, and trying to predict what might tip me over the edge was all part of the mix.

Friendships are special in life. I had good friends all around me as a young adult. They stood by me, as I was working things out. Mental illness just had not featured for many of my friends and was rarely spoken of. Young adult years are bursting with new insights, and I was grateful that I was not made to feel abnormal by my peers. I never felt threatened or labelled. I was still Mitch, who had just survived a massive "wipe-out." I remember many conversations, trying to explain what had happened, and sharing the newfound insights I had into mental illness.

Where the major challenges came about was mainly in the areas of work and study. These were made difficult due to the input of some ignorant people, belonging to the adult world. If I were to be reminded of the stigma of having a mental illness, it was in these cruel contexts where a handful of adults threw some harsh blows. I chose not to dwell on such experiences and would only go to say that the hurt that I experienced has gone on to make me the stronger person I am today.

Until someone comes to understand another who experiences mental ill health, perhaps the ability to process such affliction is limited. But it did become exhausting. I still do not understand within the adult world where the fear of "other" comes from. It is ironic that in my teens and early adult experience, it was older adults that demonstrated the most negative reactions and caution when it came to understanding my mental illness. Discrimination then usually followed. So, the stigma I experienced was perpetrated by ignorant adults, as I moved through the "troubled teen" and adult years. Most of the time, I was resilient, but I knew I would need to be robust and protect myself from discrimination and potential hurt.

Language became important as people tried to define me, and my "incapacities." Such language as asylum, mental institution, mental hospital, or psychiatric ward still conjures up for me imagery consisting of gloomy, prison-like buildings, where lunatics behaving badly are detained. Harsh treatments to rid disease of society's outcasts are performed. My history class at high school, and images portrayed within popular movies, were inaccurate and limiting.

When on trips to Sydney city, in my mother's car, from the back seat I looked on with imagination of what might take place in such archaic buildings. We would pass the grounds of one of these institutions, which were instantly recognisable by the architecture alone. The big buildings stood lonely. Isolated from surrounding landscapes. These hospitals, and the massive grounds they occupied, were places of mystery. Stories circulated through various means, all contributing to a fictional exaggeration of what these places were. I did not know anybody from my family who had been exposed to such places. So, the asylum life was largely left to the imagination.

Australian mental institutions throughout history have provided the care and treatments of the mentally ill, where people deemed unfit to participate in the normal functions of society were housed. These institutions were seen as places of safety for the individuals who resided there, and a place safely away from the day-to-day functions of civilian life.

The publication *Finding Sanity*, a biography on Dr John Cade, provides an intriguing and accurate picture of Victorian asylums in the 1940s. It is a unique and personal story of one individual who changed the history of psychiatry. Using lithium to treat bipolar conditions, Dr John Cade shared a close doctor-patient relationship.

When I read this book, there was evidence of community, a shared refuge for the mentally afflicted, sheltering from a daunting, hostile society. The way we treat people living with mental health in the twenty-first century in Australian society is different to the above-mentioned times of the asylum. The conditions of such institutions are usually a thing of the past. What remains in some states of Australia is the heritage listed architecture of such institutions, stemming from as early as the 1800s. Ghostly reminders of the past for some.

I want to put in context my "home away from home" experiences, the hospitalisations as a result of living with mood swings, as I attempted to find balance. I found that I was now becoming a frequent user of hospitals! Ironically, I did learn to know when it was right to go to hospital, and how to listen to my body. From these admissions to hospital, I found instant community when admitted each time to the ward. There were only a couple of instances when my voluntary admission was "involuntary"—that is, when I was scheduled by my psychiatrist.

Often my arrival was a welcome relief for me. Particularly because I would arrive with restlessness and energy. Thoughts in overload mode, I was severely elated. This was a place of safety now, and I needed to be contained, and rest. Earlier, I described my first experience of a state hospital, which was frightening. Memories of this presentation have stuck with me throughout my life. Overwhelmingly though, these admissions have been positive experiences. Always confronting, and difficult to deal with at the time, each hospital stay bought a new level of learning. I can reflect on such memories as being part of my education, and the journey of managing a lifelong condition.

Being on the inside of a psychiatric hospital ward through my juvenile years was a steep learning curve. But it all became more familiar as time went on. I can honestly say that by the time for me to go to hospital was confirmed, I was ready to go most times. I was often the one to instigate my admission. The feeling of elation and then mania is also life-threateningly scary when on the mood swing roller-coaster ride. When experiencing a manic phase, every part of me feels like it is burning up. There is energy pulsating throughout my whole body. The body may shake and there are massive butterflies in the stomach. If you have experienced a wave of adrenaline pass through you, then imagine that sensation escalating with no sense of stopping.

My thoughts race, my speech is pressured, anything and everything is achievable, in my mind. There are no barriers in life. I may be in direct communion with God or see myself as divine. I am the special one. I think I am so productive, which in the beginning might have an element of truth, however, in a manic phase, things escalate very quickly. Soon my efforts are very unproductive, though I cannot see that. I begin to lose touch with reality, and burnout is inevitable at this rate. My ability to make rational decisions diminishes quickly.

While seventeen, on an early trip to work, I found myself pulling into a car dealership off Parramatta Road in Sydney. I had all the sane intentions of buying a new Toyota Landcruiser FJ40 4x4. This was not a normal activity to undertake on a weekday prior to commencing work for the morning. I got as far as signing the contract for the car, and an application for finance.

I found my way back to work. With a sympathetic approach and kind words, my boss put me on the phone to my family. I was oblivious to anything going on. Luckily for me, on this occasion, my family were contacted prior to me getting to work that morning by the car salesman. He had called to verify the deal. Needless to say, the 4x4 deal was off.

As my manic state was in full swing, the alarm bells were ringing for those around me. I could hear them too. But they would not have been as loud to me. There was some reluctance for me to surrender at this point, as I was simply feeling great. Luckily, on this occasion, I could still listen to reason. The next step was a phone call to my doctor, made by Mum. A voluntary admission to hospital followed. Back to the safe house again.

My family were ever ready to back me up through such trials during these periods. I will never know what pain they went through. But in my normal states of sanity, I have most always appreciated their love and devotion to my cause. The hospital staff were that front line when, through the doors, these "special ones" like me would burst. The signs of an escalating mania are not hard to miss. Whether by voluntary admission, brought in by a family member, or the scheduled arrival by ambulance, the hospital staff had a special knack of gently accepting me into their fold.

Often, my over exuberant friendliness meant I hit it off with people. I would ensure that I connected with every nurse, doctor, cleaner and patient. I can remember trying to be very helpful in the healing of other patients on many occasions in my euphoric states. Swift intervention by the staff was not lacking when I would be in this elated or manic phase. The administration of the appropriate medication management would be established, for the benefit of all!

In the first instance, what was required was to reduce the "high." An untreated manic phase can quickly lead to a psychosis. Being out of touch with reality can be fatal. I could then quickly become exhausted. The only thing that would follow this state is the crash and burn. Like the flicking of a switch, the mood state changes. Body fatigue, depression, collapse and down time follows. From the escalating high, to the days and weeks, even months, of a low.

What I've described in this section was the new normal

for me. As you can imagine, it did make for a very disruptive period of my life. All I was endeavouring to do was to get ahead. It did seem two steps forward, one step back a lot of the time. I have always been one to look on the positive though. I was now living and making choices in all areas of life. I had many starts and stops, but I always seemed to land on my feet. I was taking control, of what I could.

I began talking about community, and the hospital experience for me being a safe place. It was a "home away from home," as mentioned. I resided with other people who were living with mental health affliction as well. There was always a sense of camaraderie among people in these environments. I have heard of many people's personal stories over the years, of the recovery journeys that individuals and families have experienced. I have shared some laughs and shed many a tear along the way with others.

I soon became familiar with my own recovery story. I found comfort in knowing that I was part of a community of "others," no matter what diagnosis.

A family friend from my sailing days assisted me to find a suitable boat building company. He was on standby over the months. It took two more work experiences before I landed the right fit. My newfound boss was the supportive mentor. Witchcraft Motor Cruisers was a wonderful training ground as a young apprentice boat builder. I began developing my craft as an apprentice boat builder among a fine team of tradesman. I was involved in all aspects of the boat construction and civil public works contracts, from sweeping the floors to laying up the fiberglass mould, the fit-out procedure, or slipping the final twenty-four foot Motor Cruiser unit. My attendance at TAFE complemented my learning.

It was not all smooth sailing though. Every couple of months, during the next eighteen-month period, were troublesome with my moods. The lithium ended up not being able to do the whole job of keeping me stable. I would first experience an elevation in mood. Eventually my mood would change from good to great, then soar to extremely fantastic. Things would get way over the top. Exhaustion, shut down, with the use of added mood stabilisers and anti-psychotic medication. Then crash. Like a switch had been flicked again. I would slump into a depression swing. Weeks spent in bed. Devastating, and very disruptive to anything going on in my life. This pattern would repeat itself for a long time. No relief from the patterns of living a roller-coaster life.

Eighteen is marked with new responsibilities. Some we are aware of; others may not really be understood until we get there. At the age of eighteen, voting age, informed or not with the political process, this marks an important step in an individual's life. It is likely that the hereditary adult world handed down to us contains a portion of our parents' views on such political persuasions. Then again, as people in our late teens, we may also radically have opposed our parents on many fronts, including political ideologies.

The list of new experiences by this stage of late teens has most likely included a heart-breaking relationship (or a few), handling money, obtaining a license, study, work, some travel, among other things. Peer pressure remains. At eighteen, many young adults are becoming determined in their own destiny. Retrospectively, I trolled through my own journals and reminisced on many of the activities, fun adventures, misadventures, and life-learning experiences. I would not wish bipolar on anybody, and turmoil takes years to tame. Psychosis and mood swings are no easy ride, but finding true balance is the name of the game.

I have been asked by friends if I would change anything in my years living with bipolar. I think consistently my response has been "no." I think that I have followed through with the comment that I would not necessarily want to do it again, as I did have major struggles during those years. The events and memories of my youth remain important, for reasons only known to me. I have lived the highs and lows to the fullest extremes. I can now say that in a calm and grounded mood too. I began journaling from this period of eighteen. This "life stage" of seventeen to eighteen was, in many ways, made easier through the therapeutic process of writing.

I now think I know what was behind the decision to commit to this cathartic process of writing. I owned and committed to it for my own healing, and to make my own voice heard, by recording life for myself. The many workings out that have taken place, and still do, have gone a long way to affirming myself. There, deep down inside, has been this little voice that has desired to speak out. It now can be listened to and heard.

I was encouraged to see things like taking the little frightened child or teen and putting him up on my shoulder. Let him see the world from my determined adult advantage point. Writing about what I did see was all important now from an adult's viewpoint. To say, "Hey, it is alright now," empowered that little one. From a safe perspective I can say it really is okay now. There is a whole world out there worth exploring. I did this in my early adult years, and it provided wonder, adventure, joy, and sometimes pain. I just thought to myself, I can give it a go.

Writing about my troubles was a decision of my own. I chose to proceed and record my thoughts. This informal approach with no rules to writing helped enormously. Where I do need to say special thanks though, is to a dear friend and mentor: a psychologist who helped me see this process through. He had belief in me and helped me to realise my inner dreams. He encouraged me to take heart, and step courageously into the future.

He would often remind me, when I needed to hear it, that I was a resilient child growing up, and this helped me to shine into my early adult years. "It's not your fault," he often reminded me. My self-esteem suffered growing up living under the diagnosis of bipolar, and this label certainly humbled the teen in me. I did feel small inside myself for many years but over time, with help, I grew in confidence. I embraced the challenge of life. I learnt to stride out, not fearing to stumble, which I did on many occasions. But I would always "pick myself up, dust myself off, and start all over again."

14
The Golden Fleece of Wellbeing

I had now well and truly concluded my adolescent years and launched into a new beginning, fully acknowledging my situation. Eighteen in our culture is seen as quite a milestone. I embraced the adult in me with both hands. I think everyone relaxes a bit each year following. So it was in my family. I had proven that I had managed to transition into adulthood quite well, despite all the obstacles. For most people, I presume, along the way, the bubble gets burst. We arrive at an understanding of our own identity that we have ourselves sculpted. The hope is to arrive at an honest understanding of self. For now, I had arrived in knowing myself. Truthfully.

My eighteenth year was a year of consolidation. I was blessed with a close friendship and worked hard at keeping an even keel across all life domains. My faith had never been stronger, and I had purpose. I was enjoying life, travels, friendships, church life and my work endeavours.

The year rolled on, as I explored all possibilities. I had connected with a solid group of guys. A few of them fellow surfers, but definitely all of them adventurous and strong in their own ways and deeply dedicated in their Christian faith. We were all determined in our own unique way. The future was looking bright. Many of my mates were at university studying their undergraduate degrees. During the semester breaks we would descend upon the South Coast for a surfing safari for a few days at a time. We all were involved in what was known as a "Beach Mission" over the Christmas break. A wonderful time of learning, sharing, and living out our faith within the local communities on the coast. Nowra was a particularly special destination. Rolling green mountain ranges and offering great surf breaks all around the region.

At the age of nineteen, I would not say that I had everything together. I had matured along the way, as a result of the challenges I had overcome, but I think, importantly, I was able to swallow the pride of my younger days.

Responsibility for myself was harnessed with the real acknowledgment that I would most likely need some form of medication management for the rest of my life. I do remember asking this question of my doctor. The response was a convincing yes, if I was to succeed in obtaining the goals I had so readily made known to others over the last couple of years.

At that time, I literally accepted this fact, and continued with the ritual act of swallowing my pills daily, without fail. From that point on, this act of self-care would not be something I would hate doing. I could not sustain that kind of attitude after all. Rather I saw this daily decision as a means of allowing me to achieve all my desires in life. I wanted balance, not the overwhelming roller-coaster ride. I had many plans for my life at such a tender adult age.

I never had anyone who I respected tell me I could not do the things I dreamed. Our choices enable us to achieve the things we ultimately want to do. Our abilities get us there. We first need to know we can do it. By making our dreams and goals known, we work at strategies for each step along the way. I realised that I needed others to help me get where I wanted to be. Before I knew it, I had such a network. My mother's intervention as a parent and carer enabled me to form the attitude and maturity to valuing my health. I adopted my own practice of questioning my ongoing treatment. I built a dedicated support network. This consisted of a genuine GP, psychiatrist, psychologist, ministers of faith, and a community of friends. My family have always been on board.

We attain self-determination in order to survive. Finding the ability to go on, as the struggle is always constant, is about finding our own story, being proud of it, and letting it be known. That is where the affirmation is key. Some of us need an audience, others work it out in other ways. We all need to be listened to, and heard, in the unique way that makes us, us. And the way that this takes place comes through many various forms of expression, from those baby cries, to adult moans and groans, and screams of laughter too.

Shakespeare indeed was right when he said that "life is a stage." Erickson stated and theorised it too. Dorothy ultimately did in the finding of wisdom. On the stage of her journey where she pushes the Wizard to the side. The auditioning is derived from the world around us, as we bustle to explore life in this busy world. We want to see where we might just fit in, and which roles we are most suited to act out.

In the 1980s there was an advertisement for a popular paint brand. As a creative person and painter, and from a marketing point, it won me over. The point is that we indeed paint our own picture of life. We need to get creative with the "stuff of me." My house, if you remember from the opening chapters in this book, is the metaphorical making of myself, or you, and your house. In the paint commercial mentioned above, someone who has just completed painting their own house sings for joy, at the completion of the project.

To live both through the comedy and tragedy is my way,

if indeed it is the way. The script of such expression has been written for each of us to perform for the audience of life itself and interpreted and acted out as our offering contribution of opportunity given to us. Negotiating our own part and fulfilling the character we own most within the rhythm of life requires the word that I've come to embrace: participation!

To safely conclude this chapter, my reflective surf safari journal-come-manuscript draws to a close. So, back into the Woody it is. It is the return journey back down those beaten tracks, where I happily traverse those meandering avenues back to the freeway that are familiar. The experience was simply amazing. With clear vision, and a collection of memories behind me, my trip is done. The final resting point and destination for this vehicle now is that of my garage, at my home. The freeway trip home only seems to take half the time. Mostly, we just want a resting place.

My brothers have supported me all the way through my good and troubled times. We lost Stuart in the year of 1996. It was a tragedy. He would have liked to have had the opportunity years later to get to know my wife and my kids. I believe he would have participated in marriage for himself. He was a gay man without marriage opportunity, a brilliant actor, artist, musician and poet. Bless you, as you did bless us with all you gave to life. Stuart's time with us was like a bright shining star across the night sky.

Decision making rests with oneself. It is my choice if I am to own my destiny. Among community we realise a greater self, which influences choice. Let us partake in each other's stories and journeying and celebrate the highs and lows life has to offer us all each moment. Every choice is worth your while. I accept the choices I made. I encourage you to cherish the choices you make too. Find the path that is yours, as I have.

During my Fine Art coursework, I painted and constructed a picture attempting to tell the story of my journey on canvas. In it, I sought to represent a belief in myself. I had made it in life. I did hold on to the dream, which was dreamed long ago, and I did reach a point where I aspired to be whole. My painting now hangs in my garage as testament. I sign off as yours truthfully, Mitchell Bennett. An introduction into the Human Services industry has continued, and a second career path beckoned. I would grow into this one, in all its varieties over the following thirty years. Social Work.

I have provided you, the audience, the backdrop to the stuff of me. I write now as an adult, husband, dad, uncle, godfather, friend, brother, brother-in law and son, son-in-law. I have written it, through my eyes. To you, from me. "Innocence in a sense."

Acknowledgements:

The very first person who comes to mind is my mother, Jan Bennett, RIP 2015. Without her love and dedication as a carer, I would not be here to tell my story. My three brothers, John, Stuart and Andrew, who have each separately helped shape the person I am, and together made growing up a rich arena of where much creativity, testosterone and brotherly love flowed. My extended family, grandparents, uncles and aunts and cousins, who provided a supportive family context and further influenced the development of my identity growing up. I particularly thank Denise, and her family for my post-breakdown support.

My dad, the late Frank Bennett, RIP 1969. Although I was only sixteen months young when he died, I know his presence in my life was real. His life and legacy we have been reminded of throughout our lives thanks to Mum and my extended family members. And I have been able to witness his work as a journalist captured on film, thanks to the ABC archives.

My friends all the way from primary school and high school years and up. Thanks to social media, I'm connecting back with more of you all the time.

The ministers who were influential in my years growing up. There were many from varying contexts and denominations. Particularly though, a special mention of the late Rev Lach Finlay, who supported and inspired me from a young age. He also supported our family through good and not so easy times.

Dr Gary Boyle—a most remarkable mentor and psychologist who guided me for many years. I couldn't have done it all without you, mate. The whole life thing! Dr Hordern, my psychiatrist during such turbulent teen and young adult years. A sturdy conservative man, though gentle in his ways. Dr Corrigan, who has taken up the baton in later years, in the most skilled and compassionate way. I owe the recent years of stability of my moods, health and success to his wisdom and care.

And then there is Deb Boyle. Who has been a sturdy rock much in the background for many years. A kind and compassionate friend, a wise leader within a shared work context—welcoming me into the field of mental health. And editor extraordinaire. With so much patience, and no judgement, helped me craft this memoir fit for a broader audience. I am indebted to both Gary and Deb. Together they have modelled the most wonderful teamwork, love, and dedication to my family and many, many people.

To all the people I have met and journeyed with who are living with mental health affliction. Thank you for the camaraderie with casual conversations in corridors, over breakfasts, lunches, dinners, coffee breaks and support groups. You have all contributed to my growth as an individual. And, of course, there are the many dedicated nursing staff of the frequented hospitals where I have recovered on many occasions. I wish to thank each of you for your dedication and care. You know who you are.

The cleaners and caterers have also been special people when in hospital. Always up for a chat—or monologue!

The Pendergast family and all the gang for accepting me into the fold. Thank you, Pam and George. And Amanda for spurring me on with the project, once upon a time.

Sal. You fell for me. And I you. I'm sure I went first though! I am honoured over all these years to have experienced your unwaning friendship. Unconditional love. In our early days, even from reading all my journals, you still joined me at the hip! Thank you for your love and support. You are wise beyond your years. And look what we have grown!

To our boys, Aaron and Joel—they are my dream that became a reality. To have the privilege to be your dad has been truly magnificent. And a lifelong ambition. And (it ain't over yet). I dedicate this book to you both.

My Spirit God. Through Jesus Christ.

References

A Fresh Start. John Chapman. Publisher: Matthias Media, 1997.

One of Australia's foremost evangelists, John Chapman explains what a Christian is, how to become a Christian and how to begin a new life through Jesus. As a general-purpose evangelistic book for giving away, *A Fresh Start* has proven highly effective over many years.

The Power of One. Bryce Courtenay. Publisher: Penguin, 2006.

First with your head and then with your heart … so says Hoppie Groenewald, boxing champion, to a seven-year-old boy who dreams of being the welterweight champion of the world. For the young Peekay, it's a piece of advice he will carry with him throughout his life.

Finding Sanity: John Cade, Lithium and the Taming of Bipolar Disorder. Publisher: Allen & Unwin, 2016.

The first biography of the ground-breaking Australian doctor who discovered the first pharmacological treatment for mental illness. For most of human history, mental illness has been largely untreatable. Sufferers lived their lives—if they survived—in and out of asylums, accumulating life's wreckage around them.

Tranquillity Denied: Stress and Its Impact Today. Dr Anthony Hordern. Publisher: Rigby Limited, 1976.

Emotional Intelligence: Why it Can Matter More Than IQ. Daniel Goleman. Publisher: Bloomsbury Publishing, 1996.

Iron John: Men and Masculinity. Robert Bly. Publisher: Random House Australia, 1990.

The Men and The Boys. R.W. Connell. Publisher: Allen & Unwin, 2000.

Manhood: An Action Plan for Changing Men's Lives. Steve Biddulph. Publisher: Finch Publishing Sydney, 1994

Attachment and Loss. John Bowlby. Pimlico edition. Publisher: Random House, 1997

The Ryrie Study Bible. New International Version. New Testament: Romans 8:28.

"And we know that in all things, God works together for good, for those that love him, who have been called according to his purpose".

Good Will Hunting. Film directed by Gus Van Sant with Matt Damon, Ben Affleck, Stellan Skarsgård, John Mighton. Released 1998.

Will Hunting, a janitor at M.I.T., has a gift for mathematics, but needs help from a psychologist to find direction in his life.

The Lego Movie. Film: released 2014.

Calamity Jane. Film: released 1953.

The Wizard of Oz. Film: released 1939.

www.ingramcontent.com/pod-product-compliance
Lightning Source LLC
Chambersburg PA
CBHW020323010526
44107CB00054B/1950